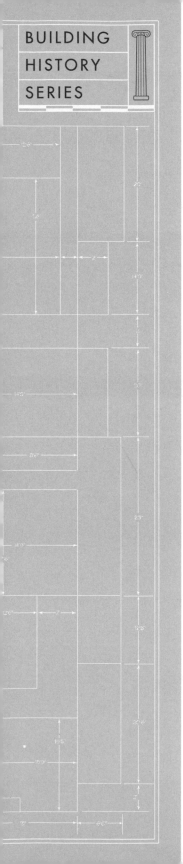

THE

PYRAMIDS

OF GIZA

THE

PYRAMIDS

OF GIZA

by Tim McNeese

Lucent Books, Inc., San Diego, California

TITLES IN THE BUILDING HISTORY SERIES INCLUDE:

The Great Wall of China
The New York Subway System
The Panama Canal
The Pyramids of Giza

Library of Congress Cataloging-in-Publication Data

McNeese, Tim.
    The pyramids of Giza / by Tim McNeese.
        p.   cm. — (Building history series)
    Includes bibliographical references (p.   ) and index.
    Summary: Describes the construction of the three great pyra-
mids on the Giza Plateau near the edge of Egypt's Western
Desert.
    ISBN 1-56006-426-9 (alk. paper)
    1. Pyramids of Giza (Egypt)—Design and construction—
Juvenile literature.   2. Building—Egypt—Juvenile literature.
[1. Pyramids—Egypt. 2. Egypt—Antiquities.] I. Title.   II. Series.
DT63.M35   1997
690'.68'0932—dc21   96-45622
                                                                    CIP
                                                                     AC

Copyright 1997 by Lucent Books, Inc.
P.O. Box 289011, San Diego, California 92198-9011

Printed in the U.S.A.

CONTENTS

FOREWORD

Throughout history, as civilizations have evolved and prospered, each has produced unique buildings and architectural styles. Combining the need for both utility and artistic expression, a society's buildings, particularly its large-scale public structures, often reflect the individual character traits that distinguish it from other societies. In a very real sense, then, buildings express a society's values and unique characteristics in tangible form. As scholar Anita Abromovitz comments in her book *People and Spaces*, "Our ways of living and thinking— our habits, needs, fear of enemies, aspirations, materialistic concerns, and religious beliefs—have influenced the kinds of spaces that we build and that later surround and include us."

That specific types and styles of structures constitute an outward expression of the spirit of an individual people or era can be seen in the diverse ways that various societies have built palaces, fortresses, tombs, churches, government buildings, sports arenas, public works, and other such monuments. The ancient Greeks, for instance, were a supremely rational people who originated Western philosophy and science, including the atomic theory and the realization that the earth is a sphere. Their public buildings, epitomized by Athens's magnificent Parthenon temple, were equally rational, emphasizing order, harmony, reason, and above all, restraint.

By contrast, the Romans, who conquered and absorbed the Greek lands, were a highly practical people preoccupied with acquiring and wielding power over others. The Romans greatly admired and readily copied elements of Greek architecture, but modified and adapted them to their own needs. "Roman genius was called into action by the enormous practical needs of a world empire," wrote historian Edith Hamilton. "Rome met them magnificently. Buildings tremendous, indomitable, amphitheaters where eighty thousand could watch a spectacle, baths where three thousand could bathe at the same time."

In medieval Europe, God heavily influenced and motivated the people, and religion permeated all aspects of society, molding people's worldviews and guiding their everyday actions. That spiritual mindset is reflected in the most important medieval structure—the Gothic cathedral—which, in a sense, was a model of heavenly cities. As scholar Anne Fremantle so elegantly phrases it, the cathedrals were "harmonious elevations of stone and glass reaching up to heaven to seek and receive the light [of God]."

Our more secular modern age, in contrast, is driven by the realities of a global economy, advanced technology, and mass communications. Responding to the needs of international trade and the growth of cities housing millions of people, today's builders construct engineering marvels, among them towering skyscrapers of steel and glass, mammoth marine canals, and huge and elaborate rapid transit systems, all of which would have left their ancestors, even the Romans, awestruck.

In examining some of humanity's greatest edifices, Lucent Books' Building History Series recognizes this close relationship between a society's historical character and its buildings. Each volume in the series begins with a historical sketch of the people who erected the edifice, exploring their major achievements as well as the beliefs, customs, and societal needs that dictated the variety, functions, and styles of their buildings. A detailed explanation of how the selected structure was conceived, designed, and built, to the extent that this information is known, makes up the majority of the volume.

Each volume in the Lucent Building History Series also includes several special features that are useful tools for additional research. A chronology of important dates gives students an overview, at a glance, of the evolution and use of the structure described. Sidebars create a broader context by adding further details on some of the architects, engineers, and construction tools, materials, and methods that made each structure a reality, as well as the social, political, and/or religious leaders and movements that inspired its creation. Useful maps help the reader locate the nations, cities, streets, and individual structures mentioned in the text; and numerous diagrams and pictures illustrate tools and devices that bring to life various stages of construction. Finally, each volume contains two bibliographies, one for student research, the other listing works the author consulted in compiling the book.

Taken as a whole, these volumes, covering diverse ancient and modern structures, constitute not only a valuable research tool, but also a tribute to the human spirit, a fascinating exploration of the dreams, skills, ingenuity, and dogged determination of the great peoples who shaped history.

IMPORTANT DATES IN THE BUILDING OF THE PYRAMIDS OF GIZA

ca. 2640
Construction of the Medum pyramid.

ca. 2200–2050
First Intermediate period marked by governmental collapse, repeated warfare, and famines across Egypt.

B.C.
ca. 3100–2686
Egyptian royalty are buried in brick mastabas.

ca. 2613–2589
The Bent Pyramid at Dahshur is constructed during Snefru's reign.

ca. 1800–1570
Second Intermediate period marked by the invasion of the foreigners, the Hyksos, who ruled northern Egypt.

| B.C. 3000 | 2750 | 2500 | 2250 | 2000 | 1750 | 1500 | 1250 | 1000 |

ca. 2700
Egyptians develop mummification.

ca. 2550–2470
The three Pyramids at Giza are built by pharaohs Khufu, Khafre, and Menkaure.

ca. 1570–1085
Pharaohs rely less on pyramids and create burial sites in the rock tombs of the Valley of the Kings.

ca. 2686–2613
Sakkara Step Pyramid is constructed.

ca. 2050–1800
Middle Kingdom; a prince of Thebes reunites the cities and rulers of the Egyptian lands.

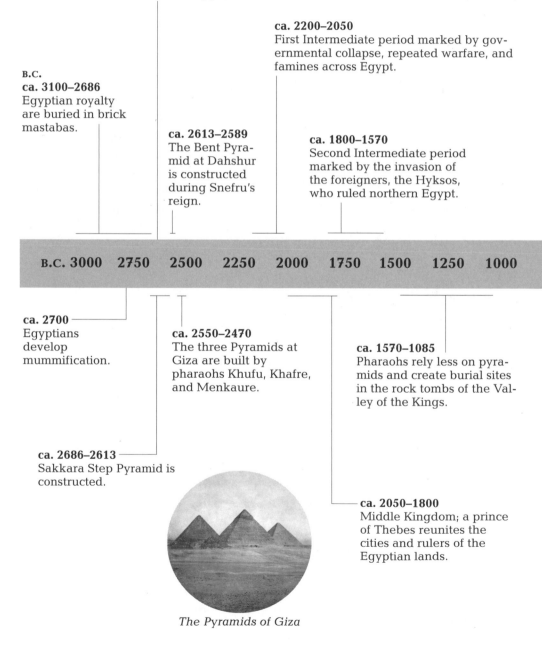

The Pyramids of Giza

8

The Great Sphinx

1954
Archaeologists discover a great funeral boat buried next to the Great Pyramid of Khufu to provide the pharaoh transportation in the afterlife.

1837–1838
British archaeologist Richard Howard-Vyse discovers the burial chamber of pharaoh Menkaure.

Early 1500s
Turks invade Egypt and use the Great Sphinx for target practice for their cannon.

A.D. 800   1300   1800   1850   1900   1950   2000

1880–1914
Noted English Egyptologist Flinders Petrie directs archaeological excavations at Giza.

**A.D.
800s**
Al-Mamun and an expedition of scientists, architects, engineers, and workers explore the Pyramids of Giza; his team breaks into Khufu's pyramid, discovering the empty burial chamber of the pharaoh.

1990s
Nearly 2 million tourists visit the Pyramids of Giza annually.

1818
Burial chamber of pharaoh Khafre is discovered by European pyramid explorer Giovanni Belzoni.

INTRODUCTION

For centuries people all over the world have marveled at the existence of great stone monuments, called pyramids, that were built thousands of years ago. These ancient structures come in many different shapes and sizes. Some were built as tombs for important kings. Others served as temples where sacrifices, including human sacrifice, took place. Such ancient pyramids were often made of stone, while others were built out of brick or even as mounds of earth.

The greatest examples of ancient pyramid building stand on the Giza Plateau, located on the fringe of Egypt's Western Desert. Three great pyramids rise hundreds of feet tall, dominating the landscape of the Nile Valley, west of Cairo, Egypt's capital. The Pyramids of Giza were built over forty centuries ago, yet they still mystify and amaze people worldwide. Historian Barbara Mertz, in her book *Temples, Tombs and Hieroglyphs*, writes:

> The pyramid form has a certain austere [harsh] beauty, and the tawny gold of the stone is capable of bewitching and subtle variations in color as the sunlight changes. But it is not the aesthetic qualities of the Great Pyramid which have hypnotized so many people. Partly, it is the size—two and one-half *million* blocks of stone, averaging two and a half tons each, comprising a structure which covers an area equal to the combined base areas of the cathedrals of Florence, Milan, St. Peter's, St. Paul's *and* Westminster Abbey.

The Pyramids of Giza are not just great mountains of stone. They are sacred burial tombs for three Egyptian pharaohs and the centerpieces of an elaborate complex that includes smaller pyramids for wives and nobles.

Construction of these pyramids required much planning and design; careful building and engineering; highly sophisticated mathematics, including advanced geometry; and thousands of workers laboring under a burning desert sun. For each pyramid ancient Egyptians quarried millions of limestone blocks, each weighing several tons. They also had to move these blocks from the quarry to the building sites, often hundreds of miles away. Since ancient Egyptians did not have use of the wheel, moving such blocks required the backbreaking efforts of tens of thousands of workers. These ancient stones were cut so perfectly that once they were fitted together, a knife blade could not be slipped between them.

The labor that went into the building of the pyramids was as important as the finished structure, for the ancient Egyptians viewed the pharaohs as gods and the work of building their tombs as holy. The British author P. H. Newby, who has written extensively about Egyptian life, describes the primary reason why such pyramids as those at Giza were built:

> It is a mistake to regard the Pyramids as elaborate follies built for the gratification of the king and resented as such by the hundreds of thousands of laborers who sweated over the years to build them. The work was holy. The building expressed the way ancient Egyptians understood the cosmos [universe]. The worthwhileness

The Pyramids of Giza, built over four thousand years ago, remain shrouded in mystery and continue to intrigue and amaze millions of visitors each year.

of such work would have been no more questioned than, to the Christian mind, was the building of the great cathedrals in the Middle Ages.

So much went into the construction of these great towers of stone that they have long been considered one of the seven wonders of the ancient world. To be included in such a list of building monuments is even more impressive considering the Pyramids of Giza are the only one of the seven ancient wonders that still stand today.

BUILDING UP FROM THE DESERT FLOOR

The pyramid form, so magnificent in its presentation at Giza, evolved over hundreds of years. It began, archaeologists believe, with a simple mud brick structure known as a mastaba. Like later pyramids, the flat, rectangular mastaba also served as a royal tomb. Eventually it gave way to a larger tomb, essentially one mastaba built on top of another. This structure came to be known as a step pyramid because each new layer was smaller than the one below it, leaving the impression of steps. These ancient royal tombs are named for the rectangular mud brick benches found beside many houses in Egyptian villages. Although many mastabas have disappeared in the windblown sands of ancient Egypt, archaeologists have to date uncovered examples that range in size from twenty to one hundred feet in length and eight to twelve feet in height. A third form, called a bent pyramid, marked the last stage leading to development of the classic pyramid—a structure with triangular sides that rise to a peak from a square, rectangular or triangular base.

Archaeologists trace construction of the mastaba to 2686 B.C. and the reign of a pharaoh named Aha. This mastaba is part of a burial complex located in the necropolis, or cemetery, at Sakkara (also spelled Saqqara), located on the western bank of the Nile, south of Giza. Archaeologist W. B. Emery excavated this site for over twenty years, between 1935 and 1956. His work led him to link this mastaba to Aha and his time period.

The typical mastaba consisted of underground and above-ground chambers, with mud brick walls enclosing the above-ground portion of the tomb. It was common to have five chambers underground, including a room in the center for the

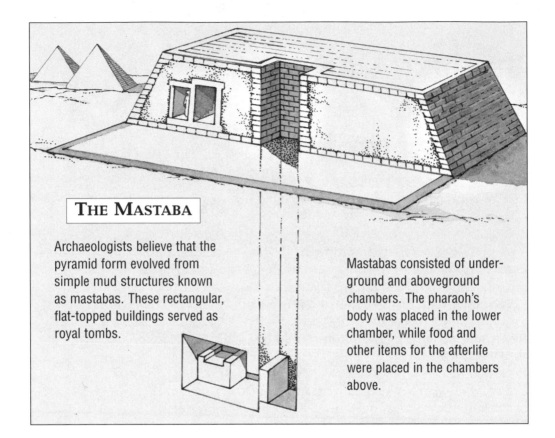

THE MASTABA

Archaeologists believe that the pyramid form evolved from simple mud structures known as mastabas. These rectangular, flat-topped buildings served as royal tombs.

Mastabas consisted of underground and aboveground chambers. The pharaoh's body was placed in the lower chamber, while food and other items for the afterlife were placed in the chambers above.

pharaoh's body, and twenty-seven chambers aboveground. These twenty-seven chambers were lined up in three rows of nine chambers each. Food for the deceased person's afterlife was stored, along with weapons and utensils, in these chambers. Some of the rooms were provided for the pharaoh's servants, who were buried in the mastaba with their king, in the belief that they would be needed to serve him in the afterlife. They were not buried alive, however; probably they were given a lethal dose of poison once they took their places in the tomb with their dead master.

THE STEP PYRAMID AT SAKKARA

Over time the design of the mastaba began to change. To make themselves even grander tombs, the pharaohs enlarged the mastabas, building new layers on top of the original tombs. The resulting structure, with each layer a little smaller than the one below it, left the impression of steps. Such pyramids came to be known as step pyramids. The earliest known step pyramid was constructed at Sakkara, just to the south of Giza. This pyramid became the tomb of pharaoh Zoser (sometimes spelled Djoser), the first pharaoh of the Third Dynasty.

The Sakkara Step Pyramid was built about 2680 B.C. under the guidance of the great Egyptian architect Imhotep. Imhotep was skilled in architecture, mathematics, and medicine and held the high-ranking government position of grand vizier. His importance in Egyptian society is demonstrated by an inscription found in one of the ceremonial courts built outside the Step Pyramid. The inscription reads: "Chancellor of the King of Lower Egypt, First after the King of Upper Egypt, Administrator of the great Palace, Hereditary Nobleman, High Priest of Heliopolis, Builder, Sculptor and Maker of Vases in Chief."

The Step Pyramid ranks high among Imhotep's many achievements. It represents Imhotep's willingness to experiment, not only with a new design, but also with the materials used in its construction. The Step Pyramid, which still stands today, consists of six mastabas set on top of each other. It measures approximately 413 by 344 feet at the base and towers more than 200 feet above the desert sand floor. The Step Pyramid was larger than any Egyptian building built before it. In addition, the pyramid was the centerpiece of a greater building project. The pyramid was surrounded by a limestone wall, nearly a mile in total length, measuring approximately 1,600 feet by 800 feet and 33 feet high. Inside the wall surrounding Zoser's pyramid, Imhotep's builders constructed smaller mastabas for royal family members, other nobility, and court advisers.

Egyptians built the Step Pyramid at Sakkara as a tomb for Third Dynasty pharaoh Zoser, pictured here in a stone relief.

Most important to the building of the Step Pyramid was its stone exterior. Before the Step Pyramid, Egyptian builders had used mud bricks for walls, and stone for floors and doorposts. Imhotep's decision to build a pyramid completely out of stone makes its construction the first of a long series of stone mastabas and pyramids. The stones Imhotep used were small compared to those later used to build the Pyramids of Giza, probably because smaller stone blocks were easier for these early builders to work with and to transport.

Imhotep's work with stone on monuments such as the Sakkara Step Pyramid won him a place in the memory of the Egyptian people as one of Egypt's first architects to build great monuments of stone. The Step Pyramid and Zoser's funerary complex at Sakkara involved the quarrying, transporting, and dressing, or smoothing, of at least one million tons of stone, mostly limestone, with pink granite used to line Zoser's burial chamber.

Just how the Step Pyramid of Zoser was built is not known. Certainly Imhotep, as well as his fellow engineers and architects, relied on building techniques that preceded this particular project. These construction methods relied heavily on hand labor during all phases of construction. The ancient Egyptians had no equipment associated with modern building techniques. They did not have the use of pulley systems, for example, which would today be considered essential for the lifting and placing of heavy limestone blocks. Archaeologists speculate that the Zoser pyramid required a permanent, skilled workforce of five thousand to ten thousand quarrymen, cutters, and masons, with an additional fifty thousand unskilled workers laboring at least part of each year of construction. Archaeologists estimate that these workers built the Zoser pyramid in less than a generation, or approximately twenty to twenty-five years.

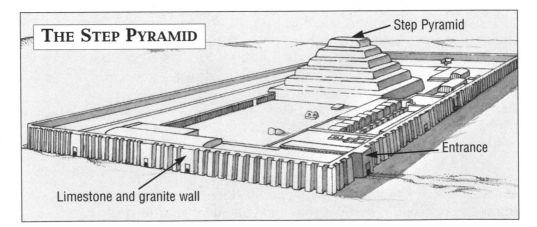

THE STEP PYRAMID

Step Pyramid

Entrance

Limestone and granite wall

The Step Pyramid of Zoser, so named because of its stairlike appearance, is the oldest surviving stone structure in the world. Archaeologists estimate that its construction took at least twenty years.

THE PYRAMID AT MEDUM

The step pyramid formed a bridge from the simple mastaba to the more complex true pyramid. One step pyramid was even transformed into a true pyramid through a series of structural changes. Little remains of that structure today but archaeologists have pieced together many details of its construction. The Medum pyramid was built at the end of the Third Dynasty of Egypt—about 2640 B.C.—about thirty miles south of Egypt's ancient capital of Memphis. A pharaoh named Huni, the last of the Third Dynasty pharaohs, may have been the builder of this pyramid. The pyramid at Medum is actually

IMHOTEP: EGYPT'S GREATEST ARCHITECT

With many of Egypt's monuments, the names of the men who served their pharaohs as architects are lost in the mists of history. But the name of the architect who pioneered the pyramid form in ancient Egypt is one that has stood the test of time. Imhotep carried many titles in life, including overseer of works for Zoser during the Third Dynasty of the Old Kingdom, which dates from the 2600s B.C. His step pyramid design was a highly creative effort and is still considered a major engineering feat today, given the primitive technology of his day. His reputation continued to serve him thousands of years after his death, as later Egyptians gave him honor as not only a master builder, but also as a master physician and wise man. He was eventually deified, worshiped by Egyptians. By elevating the memory of Imhotep to the status of a god, the Egyptians gave him an honor reserved only for their great pharaohs. In addition, later generations of Greeks and Romans recognized his godlike status. He became their patron god of medicine.

Little is known about this amazing Egyptian personality. So grand was his reputation that some more modern scholars came to doubt his existence. However, archaeological work has since unearthed a statue base found in the Step Pyramid of Zoser that bears Imhotep's name. Archaeologists may, in fact, have discovered his tomb. In 1956 Professor W. B. Emery led a team of archaeologists digging in the tombs

three pyramids in one. The earliest of the three is a seven-level step pyramid, rising to a height of about 180 feet. A second step pyramid was built on top of the first, adding eight tiers and about 60 feet to its height. Finished and smoothed limestone slabs found on remnants of the two pyramids indicate that the builders intended each one to be the complete and final structure. Neither one proved to be that. At some point work on the Medum pyramid began again. The four sides were evened out and the base squared, resulting in a structure with a true pyramid shape. Egyptologist I. E. S. Edwards, in his book *The Pyramids of Egypt*, describes the transformation of the Medum pyramid:

of Sakkara. Among these burial mastabas Emery uncovered the remains of pottery dating from the Greco-Roman period. Since Imhotep had been worshiped in Greco-Roman times, Emery wondered whether he might have stumbled onto Imhotep's ancient tomb and the remains of a temple cult established in his honor. Emery, however, did not return to this burial site until 1964 to continue his work.

When work resumed there, further discoveries were uncovered. The remains of sacrificed bulls and ibis mummies pointed to rituals carried out in honor of someone very important. The ibis, a long-legged bird associated with the god Thoth, was an image adopted for the worship of Imhotep, providing another link to the ancient architect. Later discoveries at this site included chambers containing mummies of baboons, also sacred to Thoth and Imhotep. Emery's work, however, did not continue long enough for him to draw any real conclusion concerning the tomb's connection to Imhotep. He died in 1971 before his studies were completed.

Imhotep

Despite his death, archaeological work at this ancient tomb continued. No conclusive evidence has ever been uncovered linking the tomb to Imhotep. The search today continues for the tomb of this mysterious, yet extremely talented Egyptian of the Old Kingdom.

This pyramid was not . . . destined to remain as a step pyramid, although it is evident that both the seven- and the eight-stepped designs were, in their turn, intended to be final. For reasons which cannot readily be explained, the steps were filled in with a packing of local stone, and the whole structure was overlaid with a smooth facing of Tura limestone. By this means, the monument was transformed into a geometrically true pyramid.

With the building of the Medum pyramid, the Egyptians had created something new. First, the angle of the sides of this pyramid is less steep. The Medum pyramid's angle of elevation

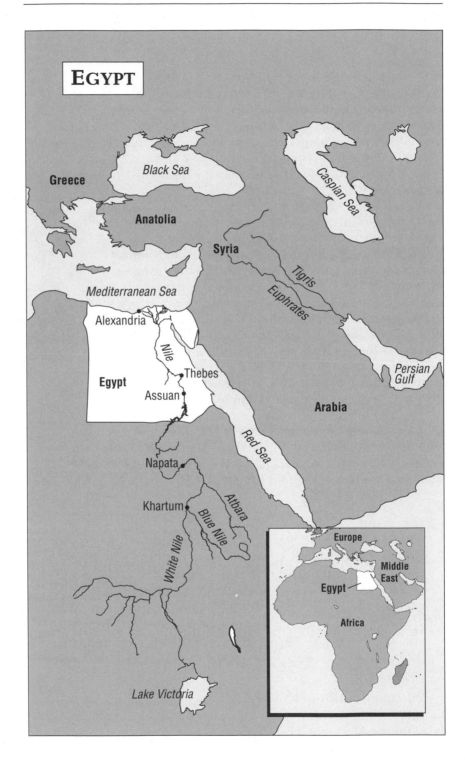

EGYPT

Greece

Black Sea

Caspian Sea

Anatolia

Syria

Tigris

Euphrates

Mediterranean Sea

Alexandria

Nile

Thebes

Egypt

Assuan

Persian Gulf

Arabia

Red Sea

Napata

Khartum

Athara

Blue Nile

White Nile

Europe

Middle East

Egypt

Africa

Lake Victoria

is fifty-two degrees. The steps of Zoser's pyramid create an angle of seventy-five degrees. Although archaeologists are unsure why the builders at Medum lowered the angle of their pyramid, such a change certainly meant that less stone would be required. Inside the Medum monument, the tomb chamber is located at the pyramid's base. This chamber may be reached by a small passageway through the pyramid that slopes at an angle of twenty-eight degrees. Such changes as the pyramid's angle and the creating of an internal passageway pointing toward the heavens reveal the basic differences between the Zoser model and the Medum structure. These changes would provide the model for other, later pyramids, including the Pyramids of Giza.

THE MEDUM COMPLEX

The structures surrounding the Medum pyramid also represented a break in traditional pyramid-building practices up to that time. There is a wall around the pyramid, and the ruins of a small pyramid are near the larger Medum model. This smaller structure and a mortuary temple are connected by a long paved causeway, or raised street, leading down to the Nile River. Along the banks of the river the Egyptians built a structure that served as a boat dock. Since its construction, this dock has sunk into the silt and sand of the Nile. The causeway points toward the celestial pole. This complex—the dock, the causeway, the mortuary temple—provided the Egyptians with a way to bring a pharaoh's body to the temple to prepare it for burial in the great stone tomb. Such a funerary system has not been found at the Zoser Step Pyramid site.

The Medum pyramid was probably the first true pyramid ever built in Egypt, although that event occurred more by happenstance than by design. Pyramid construction passed through one more stage before making the final leap to a structure that was designed and built as a true pyramid. That stage took place about twenty-eight miles north of Medum and several miles south of Sakkara, at Dahshur. There, two pyramids, which stand less than a mile apart, mark the last stage in the transition to the true pyramid form. Archaeologists feel certain that Snefru, the first pharaoh of the Fourth Dynasty, built them both. They have uncovered inscriptions in both pyramids that mention Snefru. The first of these two monuments to be built is called the Dahshur Pyramid. The second is referred to as the Red Pyramid.

THE BENT PYRAMID AT DAHSHUR

Today the Dahshur Pyramid is often called the Bent Pyramid because when the structure was only half completed, the builders decreased the angle of the sides from about fifty-four degrees to near forty-three degrees. This change gave the pyramid its bent look. Other names for this pyramid are the False, Blunted, or Rhomboidal Pyramid. This change in the angle resulted in a final height of about three hundred feet rather than a planned peak of over four hundred feet.

Why the Egyptian builders changed the pyramid's angle is still a mystery. Some Egyptologists believe the original angle proved to be a mistake, causing the builders to change their project when half finished. Others suggest that the pyramid had to be finished in a hurry, and the angle was changed then. Noted archaeologist of the early nineteenth century J. S. Perring determined through his excavations at Dahshur in 1837 that the work done on the upper half of the Bent Pyramid was completed with less care than that of the lower half. Such a change might indicate that the pharaoh for whom the pyramid was being built died earlier than expected, causing workers to hurry their construction project along.

Even though the change in angle resulted in a smaller pyramid, the Bent Pyramid is still an impressive object. Builders used approximately three and a half million tons of stone on this pyramid. While the Bent Pyramid may look different from other true pyramids, it fit into the developing pattern of pyramid construction, which included a complex of buildings outside the pyramid. Among these later buildings were a mortuary temple and a causeway to a Nile dock. Inside the pyramid two entrance passages were built, with one pointing to the pole star.

THE RED PYRAMID

Just one mile north of the Bent Pyramid stands the Red Pyramid, or the Northern Stone Pyramid at Dahshur. It takes one of its names from its reddish colored stones, now exposed, since its outside stones were stolen long ago. This pyramid has straight sides rising to a point, making it a successful true pyramid. It was built at an angle of forty-three and a half de-grees, about the same as the upper part of the Bent Pyramid. Its base covers about 660 square yards, a larger area than that of the Bent Pyramid. It is roughly the same height as the Bent Pyramid. Its entrance passage also points to the celestial pole. It leads to three chambers, all three protected by a corbelled roof, one with layers that become narrower as the roof height increases.

The building of the Red and Bent Pyramids completed the centuries-long development of the true pyramid form in ancient Egypt and paved the way for the grandest of all of Egypt's tombs: the Pyramids of Giza.

2

THE JOURNEY TO
THE AFTERLIFE

The pharaohs of ancient Egypt were not mere kings. Although, like most kings, they controlled the government and owned all of the land, Egypt's rulers fulfilled an even higher purpose. They held the status of gods. Egyptian society viewed the pharaoh as both an earthly and spiritual leader. The pharaoh saw all, knew all, and controlled all, and his subjects worshiped him without question. "As an incarnate [human] deity he upheld the fundamental order of the universe," writes Desmond Stewart. "His practical and spiritual power merited awe, homage, and tribute."

In death, as in life, the pharaoh held a place of honor. The Egyptians believed that when living beings died, they moved on to another life, which they called the afterlife. The journey to the afterlife held special significance in the case of the pharaoh. His arrival and rebirth in the afterworld meant that he could send his blessings for prosperity and a good harvest back to his people. He embarked on this important journey from the massive stone tomb built in the shape of a pyramid. Although construction of a single pyramid took years and occupied thousands of people, its completion was never in doubt, for the work represented the sacred tie between the pharaoh and his subjects. As Desmond Stewart writes:

> In life, the kings had no need for substantial buildings or solid luxury. Palaces of mud-brick, linen robes, and wooden beds sufficed for a living Horus [a god] in a gentle, almost rainless climate. . . . Eternity lasted infinitely longer than the longest mortal life, and a house for eternity—as Egyptians called the tomb—had to be far more durable than a palace. That it would cost much labor and stone to make it durable did not seem to matter; . . . it was a place of immense importance to society.

Its purpose . . . was as functional as that of a power station, and it was contrived with as practical ends in mind. The tomb was the place in which the dead king, securely buried, could receive homage and nourishment; from it the king could make his successful journey to the afterworld and thence radiate blessings back to his people.

The afterlife, the ancient Egyptians believed, existed in a mysterious world under the land of Egypt. This world was an exact copy of Egypt. The dead would find there another Nile River. They would also find that they had the same needs in the afterlife as they did in their first life: food, drink, clothing, a bed to sleep in, even a boat to travel on the underground Nile. To prepare their pharaoh for the afterlife, the Egyptians amassed everything necessary for his trip to the Eternal. They collected food, furniture, jewelry, clothes, and more.

SPIRITS OF THE DEAD

These items assured the well-being of the soul, what the Egyptians called the *ba* and the *ka*. The Egyptians believed that each person had two souls. The *ba* was the soul of the living, the *ka* the soul that served in the afterlife. The *ba* left the body upon death but stayed nearby while the *ka* made preparations for the trip to the underworld. A passage from the Egyptian *Book of the Dead*, a collection of sayings, incantations, songs, and magic rituals, refers to these dual souls: "Your soul is in

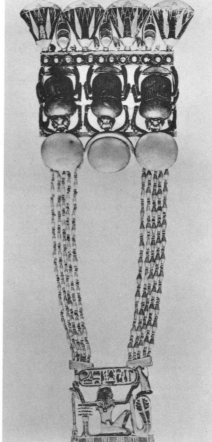

An ornate necklace found in a pharaoh's tomb. Items such as jewelry, food, and clothing were buried with the pharaohs, presumably for use in the afterlife.

heaven before [the sun god] Re; your double has what should be given to it with the gods; your spiritual body is glorious among the spirits of fire; and your material body is established in the grave."

SERVANT STATUES

It is a common myth that the Egyptian pharaohs ordered their servants to be sealed alive in the pyramids with their mummified remains so that they might continue to serve their king in the afterlife. This was not the case. Human sacrifice was not practiced in Egypt after the formation of the First Dynasty, around 3000 B.C.

Several means were used, however, to ensure that the pharaohs had servants after death. During the days of the Old Kingdom, when the Giza Pyramids were constructed, the walls of the tombs were decorated with paintings that depicted servants going about their daily activities, including cutting grain, making bread, dancing, serving food, and dressing the pharaoh. It is assumed that these painted servants would come to life when the pharaoh needed them.

In later dynasties pharaohs were buried along with small statues called *ushebtis* or *shawabtis*. These little figurines were carved from all sorts of materials, including wood and stone. These statues were also intended to come to life and perform any work assigned to the pharaoh in the afterlife. Many of the figurines were carved with instructions, explaining to the *ushebti* itself what its role was, such as the following:

> O thou ushebti! If the deceased [pharaoh] is appointed to do any work which a man does in the necropolis—to cultivate the fields, to irrigate the banks, to transport sand of the East to the West—"Here am I!" thou shalt say.

Some of the miniatures entombed with the pharaohs were not human replicas at all. These included small models of houses or boats, which would be magically enlarged to provide for the pharaoh in his new eternal existence.

During this waiting period, the *ba* lived off the food left inside the tomb's storage chambers. The *ba* might leave the tomb at night but always returned to the body of the deceased. The *ka*, however, had much more freedom. It could move back and forth between the tomb and the underworld. The *ka*'s ultimate task was to prepare a route for the final journey to the underworld. Once the *ka* had made the necessary provisions, it returned one last time to the tomb, where it joined with the *ba*. Together they set out in search of the god Osiris, the king of the dead.

JUDGMENT OF THE SOULS

The Egyptians believed that Osiris and the other gods listened to the life stories of the dead and determined whether they deserved the afterlife. The hearing took place in the Hall of Maat, the goddess of truth. In Egyptian mythology Maat took the form of an ibis, Egypt's sacred bird. To determine the truthfulness of the stories, the heart of the deceased was weighed on a balancing scale against one of Maat's feathers. If the heart was lighter than the feather, the dead person moved into the afterlife and shared eternity with relatives and friends who had already made that passage. If the heart was heavier than the feather, it was destroyed. A monster called the Devourer of Souls stood poised near the scales, watching. The devourer

Ancient Egyptians believed a dead person's heart would be weighed by the gods to determine a person's worthiness for the afterlife. At the Tribunal of the Dead, Osiris (bottom, left) waits to judge the dead, while the scales (right) are brought out to weigh the heart.

had a crocodile's head, the front body of a lion, and the back end of a hippopotamus. This creature ate all souls judged as unworthy of the afterlife.

Egyptian priests and scribes wrote sacred prayers to guide the souls of the dead in their quest for admittance to the underworld. These prayers were buried with the dead in a place where the soul could find them. Today remnants of such prayers exist in the *Book of the Dead*. One such prayer reads: "May nothing oppose me in the judgment in the presence of the Lord of the trial, Osiris. Let it be said of me, of what I have done, 'his deeds are right and true'; may nothing happen against me in the presence of the great god Osiris."

The elaborate preparations for the pharaoh's journey to the afterlife included many rituals. One of the most important was the practice of preserving the body, a process called mummification. Preservation of the body assured the *ba* of a place to stay until the journey was complete.

THE PRACTICE OF MUMMIFICATION

Mummification probably was unnecessary before the time of the pyramids. Early burial rites in Egypt simply consisted of placing a body in a shallow sand pit. There the sand dried and preserved the body before it had time to decay. This natural

An open coffin reveals the mummified remains of an Egyptian pharaoh. Mummification was an important step in the process of preparing the body for the afterlife.

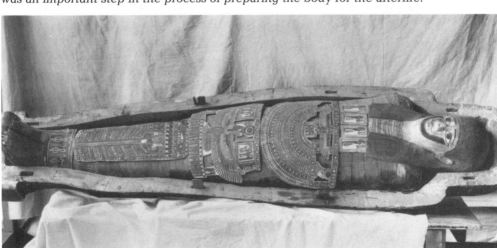

THE STORY OF OSIRIS

As did all ancient peoples, the Egyptians had many myths, legends, and stories that helped to explain the significance of their beliefs, customs, and social practices. One of the most important Egyptian myths is one about the god Osiris. This myth explains the circumstances of the afterlife and the judgment required of departed souls. It also explains why the Egyptians considered preserving a deceased pharaoh's body so important.

The story begins with Osiris, the god of fertility, and his sister-wife, Isis, goddess of nature. They ruled as the king and queen of all the Egyptian gods and goddesses. As god of fertility, Osiris shows the Egyptian people how to grow crops and plant vineyards. Osiris and Isis have a brother named Set, or Seth, the god of evil, who is very jealous of Osiris as ruler of all Egyptian deities. Set tricks Osiris into climbing inside a magic coffin, then kills him. Set then throws the coffin into the Nile River. Isis follows the coffin until it catches in the branches of a tree, but Set interferes again, this time stealing Osiris's body and cutting it into fourteen pieces, which he hides all over Egypt. Isis sets out on a search for her brother's body parts. Thoth, the god of magic and wisdom, helps Isis in her search. After finding all the pieces, Isis gives them to Anubis, the jackal god, who joins them back together.

Osiris (pictured) became god of the underworld and judge of souls after he was murdered by his jealous brother Set.

Thoth then magically revives Osiris on the condition that he remain in the spirit world. Osiris agrees and becomes the god of the underworld and grantor of eternal life. A victim of evil in his earthly lifetime, Osiris becomes the judge of good and evil in the next.

Ancient Egyptians perform the ritual of mummification. To further protect the bodies of the dead, Egyptians buried the mummies within the elusive chambers of the stone pyramids.

process could not occur once the bodies of the deceased were placed in tombs. Other means of preserving the body had to be found.

Egyptologist Barbara Mertz discusses this point:

It was logical enough that . . . the Egyptians should have turned their attention to the preservation of the body itself. The air and the soil of Egypt are in themselves excellent preservatives, and it may have been the sight of the naturally mummified bodies of the more ancient dead, baked into leather by the heated sand, that gave the early dynastic Egyptians the idea of helping the process along by artificial means. The development of civilization made artificial aids necessary; bodies laid in the sand need no other means of preservation than the heat and dryness of the medium, but when tombs were built, and the bodies of the dead were shut away from the sun, the processes of decay were unhindered.

No original Egyptian accounts of the process of mummification exist today. The writings of a few Greek historians, including Herodotus, provide some of the details. But mostly, modern-day scientists have examined the physical evidence of the mummies to discover the steps of this elaborate process, which the ancient Egyptians practiced for over three thousand years.

THE MUMMIFICATION PROCESS

The process began with the removal of the dead person's viscera, or internal organs. These organs were removed through an incision, or cut, in the stomach. The body and the organs—including the liver, stomach, lungs, and intestines—were then treated with a salt compound called natron salt or dry natron. The brain was removed through the corpse's nostrils, the embalmer using metal prongs to grab on to it and extracting the organ in pieces. The organs were then filled with bitumen—a kind of asphalt—or some other material, such as straw, sawdust or spices. Then they were wrapped and placed individually in special stone vases or jars. Called canopic jars, they were sealed and capped with a carved stopper that portrayed four Egyptian gods. This preservation process took place over a ten-week period, including about a month of religious rites and rituals.

Once the organs and the body had gone through these processes, the embalmers began wrapping the body in long strips of linen cloth. Since the linen strips were usually moistened first, they stuck closely to the body, keeping its general shape. While this process was done, more religious rituals took place, the priests singing and chanting. Occasionally a priest would slip a piece of papyrus between the layers of linen. These papyri had prayers and chants written on them. In fact, the priests had a special chant for every part of the mummified body, including the fingers and toes. Wrapping the body of a common person was done without much attention to detail. A pharaoh, nobleman, or other important person required special attention, and wrapping might take weeks or even months.

When the last linen strip was placed on the body, the body was lowered into a wooden coffin. The coffin was then set in a sarcophagus, a stone coffin, which was placed in the tomb. The sarcophagus might be decorated with figures and flowers, more prayers and animal shapes, and—especially in the case of pharaohs—a likeness of the person to show the *ba* where its body has been laid to rest.

Once the mummification process was nearly complete, the final ritual, a ceremony called Opening of the Mouth, was carried out. Its purpose was to symbolically restore the pharaoh's ability to eat and speak. The ceremony began by placing the mummy in an upright position at the door of the pyramid. A priest dressed in a leopard skin cloak, his head shaven, sprinkled the mummy with water and then sacrificed several animals. The priest then touched the mummy with a variety of special instruments, symbolically restoring the use of the pharaoh's senses and organs. Incense was burned, and religious chants spoken. With this, the process was complete. A soul had been created, symbolizing a rebirth for the pharaoh.

THE GRAND PROCESSION

On the day of the funeral a grand procession made its way toward the pyramid. The mummified remains of the pharaoh led the way, pulled on a royal sledge, or sled, by oxen or the pharaoh's male friends and relatives. The women were expected to show their emotions, mourning and grieving as the procession moved along. If a pharaoh did not have enough female family members for an adequate emotional show, professional mourners were hired. Behind the mourners came the pharaoh's servants, laden with all the items their pharaoh would need to find comfort in the afterlife: food, clothing, perfumes, furniture, weapons, and even games. Behind these items came a sledge that carried only the pharaoh's internal organs and entrails, or bowels. The procession made its way to the mortuary temple. The walls of the causeway shielded the pharaoh's coffin from the prying eyes of the outside world. This was important since the king's remains had been ritually purified and, technically, were no longer of this earth.

Once inside the mortuary temple, the priests spoke more prayers and made additional offerings to the gods. The pharaoh's coffin was then taken by the priests into the pyramid. Slowly they made their way to the burial chamber located deep within the pyramid. Once inside the chamber, the coffin was placed inside the sarcophagus and its heavy granite lid was slid into position, sealing the pharaoh's remains inside. The canopic jars containing the king's insides were placed at

A painting from an Egyptian tomb depicts servants carrying items to fill their pharaoh's tomb during the grand procession to the pyramid.

the foot of the sarcophagus. Perhaps other items—clothes, food, jewelry, and the like—were placed nearby. After final prayers, the priests left the burial chamber and sealed the access tunnels behind them.

The practice of mummification remained largely the same for hundreds of years of Egyptian practice. Details regarding how organs were removed or how the body was wrapped did change some over long, continued practice. Archaeologists can partially date mummies unearthed today by how the body was preserved. But regardless of how an Egyptian body was mummified, the corpse, along with its *ba* and *ka*, still needed a place to reside. The pyramids provided some of the most elaborate burial complexes ever constructed by Egyptians who wished their kings, their families, and their advisers a happy afterlife.

3

PREPARATION FOR
BUILDING

The age of pyramid building at Giza began with the construction of the Great Pyramid of Khufu, who ruled Egypt as pharaoh from about 2550 to 2525 B.C. As son followed father, three pyramids were built at Giza: one for Khufu (also known by the Greek name Cheops), one for his son, Khafre (also known by the Greek name Chephren), and a third for his son, Khufu's grandson, Menkaure (or Mycerinus to the Greeks). Yet construction on the plateau was not to be limited to these three great structures. These pyramids fit into a pattern already in place through the building of earlier pyramid models. The Giza Plateau is the site of literally hundreds of ruins, the most famous and obvious being the three pyramids of Khufu, Khafre, and Menkaure. Historian Desmond Stewart describes how a completed pyramid was not to be built as an isolated structure, but rather "each vast tomb was the key component, the radioactive pile, in a complex of buildings that may be understood as a spiritual reactor. The whole could not function properly without a number of important constituency [related parts]."

Generally, historians refer to the buildings that the Egyptians built around their great stone structures as the pyramid complex. This complex provided the buildings that housed the aids necessary to carry the body of a dead pharaoh on his funerary journey, with the pyramid serving as the final resting place.

In her book, *Temples, Tombs and Hieroglyphs*, Barbara Mertz, a leading authority on ancient Egypt, writes about the complex of buildings surrounding the Pyramids of Giza:

> The three great pyramids are not the only tombs at
> Giza, by a long way. There are seven smaller queens'

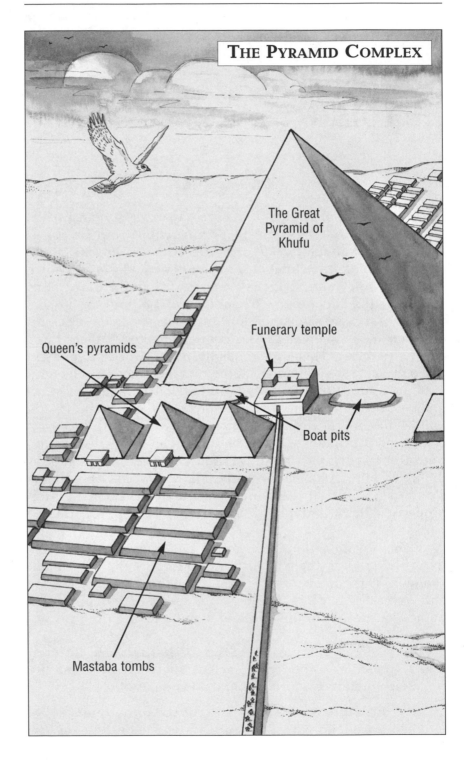

THE PYRAMID COMPLEX

The Great Pyramid of Khufu

Funerary temple

Queen's pyramids

Boat pits

Mastaba tombs

pyramids near the big ones, and there are private tombs all over the plateau. Khufu, the first king to build a pyramid at Giza, also began the private cemeteries. Wishing to ensure his numerous progeny [children] and friends a good life in the next world, he laid out a real City of the Dead, close to his pyramid so that his relatives might profit from his superior presence. The houses of the City were huge stone mastabas laid out in neat rows like city blocks. They must have looked attractive when first built, with their glistening sugar-white walls and painted offering tablets.

The whole complex of temples, chapels, and tombs scattered across the Giza Plateau was completed in less than a century and represented an enormous amount of work.

PREPARATIONS FOR BUILDING A PYRAMID

Moving gigantic stones, each weighing at least two tons, was no small effort. Yet before a single block of stone was put into place, a pyramid site had to be chosen and made level before construction could begin. Stones had to be cut, quarried, and shipped to the building site. Thousands of workers had to be assembled, each one having a specific job to carry out.

The pyramids had to be built near the Nile River because the heavy stones, supplies, and workers needed for building these monuments were transported on Nile River barges. Thus, the closer the work site was to the river, the better. The Egyptians chose the west bank of the river because the sun set in the west. According to various Egyptian myths the sun was a god who made his trip across the sky each day. One such myth describes the sky as the body of the goddess Nut, her head thought to be placed at the western horizon and her groin on the eastern. The sun was eaten by Nut each evening, traveled in darkness through the underworld, called the Det, and was then given birth from Nut's womb each morning. With each new morning the sun was reborn to shine again on his journey across the cloudless Egyptian sky. Since the sun died each evening, when consumed by Nut, the Nile's west bank became known as the Realm of the Dead.

Other factors also were considered in choosing a potential pyramid site. Pyramids might be built at a particular location because of their closeness to a pharaoh's capital or even a stone quarry. As it happens, the Giza site satisfied all the above requirements for the construction of the three immense pyramids.

THE FUNERARY COMPLEX

The three pyramids of Khufu, Khafre, and Menkaure dominate the Egyptian landscape at Giza. Yet they were not the only buildings constructed across that desert plain. They are not even the only tombs at Giza. The ruins of seven smaller pyramids, probably constructed for various queens, stand near the pharaohs' immense limestone monuments. There are still other burial buildings nearby. It was Khufu, the first pharaoh to have a great pyramid built at Giza, who ordered the laying out of a necropolis, or City of the Dead.

This consisted of tombs, seemingly endless honeycombs of mastabas, all arranged in neat rows resembling city blocks. These tombs were constructed for family and friends of the pharaoh. Originally, sixty-four such tombs were built near Khufu's pyramid.

Still other buildings, mostly in ruins today, were built at Giza as part of the pyramid complex. Each of the three Giza Pyramids of the pharaohs is part of a system connected to the funeral rituals required to entomb the three pharaohs. These buildings include the Valley Building, the dock-temple that received the royal body from a Nile River funerary barge, and a stone causeway connecting the Valley Building to the pyramid. Here the pharaoh's body was mummified and prepared for burial. At the end of the causeway stood a mortuary temple, where food, weapons, and ceremonial gear were stored for the pharaoh's use in the afterlife.

These structures, including the Valley Building and the mortuary temple, served as the sites for the ceremonies that were required to entomb each pharaoh. Their walls were usually decorated with paintings, statues, and hieroglyphs picturing the pharaoh's great deeds. Sometimes the events described never happened but were included to make the pharaoh look more heroic and majestic.

An illustration from an Egyptian mummy case portrays the goddess Nut, who, according to Egyptian myth, devoured the sun each evening and gave birth to it each morning.

LEVELING THE SITE

Also important to determining a specific site was how flat and level it was to begin with. After removing the surface sand, the workers, using copper chisels and wooden mallets, would remove the rock from a prospective site until they reached bedrock. Such a gigantic building needed a solid, permanent foundation. But hard rock was not enough for a pyramid base. No site was perfectly level naturally, so surveyors were brought in to solve the problem.

Without benefit of sophisticated tools and instruments, the surveyors instructed workers to cut a grid of interconnecting rock trenches all over the new pyramid site with their chisels and mallets. Workers then filled the network of trenches with water. Marks were made on the trench walls along the water's edge. Since the channels interconnected, the water level was the same in each trench, despite the depth of each individual trench. These marks were consistently made at the same level across the pyramid site. Once the water was drained from this complex of ditches, the workers then cut out any rock that stood above the marked water lines. The result

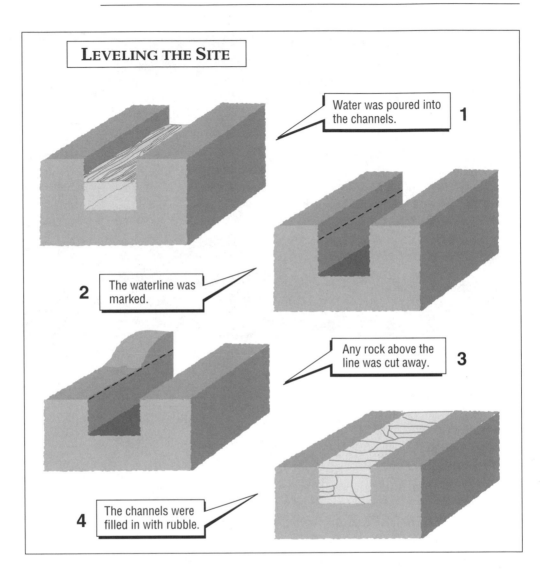

LEVELING THE SITE

Water was poured into the channels. **1**

The waterline was marked. **2**

Any rock above the line was cut away. **3**

The channels were filled in with rubble. **4**

was that all rock outcroppings were cut down to the same level, flattening out the site. The trenches were then filled in with stones, providing a flat, solid site for the construction of a giant pyramid.

This trench system was extremely successful. For example, the base of the Great Pyramid of Khufu is equal to seven and a half soccer fields. With such a large area to level, having no sophisticated instruments such as the modern surveyor's transit, how accurate were the ancient Egyptians in their efforts? The Great Pyramid is, by all modern standards, almost perfectly level. Measurements have been taken, and the southeast corner of the Khufu pyramid is only a half inch higher than the northwest corner.

ORIENTING THE PYRAMID

Leveling the site was extremely important and necessary to laying a solid foundation for a mammoth pyramid. But equally important to the pyramid builders was the exact position of the pyramid base. The Egyptians, for reasons not completely understood, built the Pyramids of Giza with each side facing the four cardinal compass points: north, south, east, and west. But just as they had no transit for surveying, they had no compass to determine true north. How was it done?

Egyptian astronomy probably helped to solve this problem. Later Egyptian texts reveal that temples were oriented by "looking at the sky, observing the stars, and turning [one's] gaze toward the Great Bear [the constellation Ursa Major, which includes the Big Dipper]." But just looking at the stars alone does not give enough accuracy to one's calculations in determining true north.

Modern scientists theorize that the Egyptians built a circular wall in the center of the planned building site. The wall had to be high enough so that the natural horizon could not be seen. It also had to be made level. The result was the creation of a man-made horizon. As night fell, a priest or a surveyor stood in the exact center of the walled circle. Facing to the east, the surveyor waited until a chosen star in the northern sky rose above the top of the wall. Armed with a forked stick called a *bay*, the surveyor marked the spot on the wall where the star had appeared. Some hours later that same star would pass below the wall, out of the observer's view. Then the surveyor, again sighting the setting star through the *bay*'s small fork, marked the place on the wall where the star disappeared from sight. Since stars look as though they rotate around the north pole, the surveyor knew that by marking a third place on the wall, halfway between the points of the rising and setting star, that mark would indicate true north. The surveyor drew a line from the first two marks on the wall into the circle's center. Bisecting this angle created a line running straight north and south. This little bit of

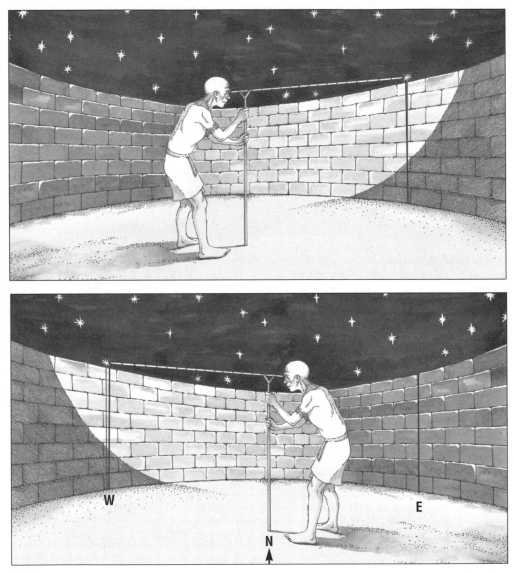

To determine true north, a surveyor or priest marked the position of a rising star in the eastern sky. Several hours later, he marked the star's position as it set. The position halfway between the rising and setting star indicated true north.

astronomical ingenuity gave the Egyptians the lines they needed to orient the pyramid base along the cardinal points of the compass.

Evidence of such astronomy practices exists in ancient Egyptian texts and in tomb drawings. Such a drawing is described in the following excerpt of an article written by Evan Hadingham for the *Atlantic* magazine:

> In a rock-cut tomb 300 feet beneath the desert near Luxor one of the earliest known Egyptian astronomical scenes, drawn in black on the ceiling, consists of a noble procession of divinities bearing sun disks on their heads. A prominent figure holds an object about the size of a tennis-racket handle at arm's length and at eye level; this object looks like a sighting instrument—perhaps the simple wooden sighting stick known to the Egyptians as a *bay*. Museum specimens and later texts suggest how the *bay* was used to make sightings of stars. A priest would peer through a small notch carved on the top of the *bay*, similar to the back sight of a rifle, until he had the star in view. To help line up the star, he used other aids, such as a plumb line suspended in front of him like a rifle's front sight. . . . Cheops's architects might well, therefore, have used sightings of stars revolving around the pole to fix their accurate north-south baseline for the pyramid. The orientation could have been checked by repeated measuring of noonday shadows cast by the sun.

Egyptians use a length of rope to survey an area. Even without sophisticated equipment, the Egyptians were able to measure precisely.

Once the side directions were determined, the Egyptians attempted to lay out the pyramid's base as a square, with all sides being equal in length. This process was difficult for the Egyptians, for they did not have any sophisticated measuring devices; not even something as simple as a metal measuring tape. What they had were palm or flax fiber measuring cords. These cords, especially when used to measure a distance as long as a side of the Great Pyramid (755 feet), easily stretched, giving the surveyors difficulties in creating a base exactly square, with each base corner a right angle. Here the Egyptians had to settle for something a little less than exact, but not by much. The greatest difference between any two sides of the Great Pyramid is a little less than eight inches!

QUARRYING AND CUTTING THE STONE

Once the pyramid site was selected, leveled, and the base squared and aligned with the compass points, it was time for the stones to be brought to the work site. Men had been hard at work in Egyptian stone quarries, cutting out the first blocks for the pyramid.

An artist's sketch depicts Egyptian workers standing among the giant blocks of limestone that will be used to construct pyramids.

Two types of stone were used in building the monuments at Giza: a soft rock called limestone, and granite, a harder form of stone. Both these stone types could be found along the banks of the Nile in the quantities needed for these mammoth buildings. Granite quarries, however, were farther from Giza than the limestone quarries, at least five hundred miles to the south. Most of the stones used at Giza were limestone, since it was easier to quarry than granite.

Quarrymen in ancient Egypt relied on few tools and lots of muscle and determination. When quarrying limestone, two methods were used: opencast and tunneling. Opencast quarrying was done when the limestone was located on the surface. Men fanned out over a large outcropping of stone and used long copper chisels and wedges to cut the blocks out. This method was easier than tunneling. However, sometimes the desired stone was located inside a cliff of stone, requiring the quarry workers to carve their way horizontally into the side of such sources.

Historian John Weeks, in his book *The Pyramids*, describes the ancient Egyptian tunnelling process of quarrying:

> When the Egyptians mined the limestone by means of tunnels . . . they first cut a hollow in the side of the cliff . . . large enough for a man to work in. The floor of the hollow would be the top of the stone the men wished to quarry. A quarryman then crawled into this hollow and using long copper chisels cut down the back and sides of the stone block. They used wooden mallets to hammer down the chisels. The block would then be free on all sides except at the bottom. Holes would then be cut at the bottom of the block and wedges driven in to make the block split away from the rock to which it was joined. Sometimes the wedges were made of wood which swelled up when soaked with water, again causing the rock to split along the bottom. Great care had to be taken at this stage or the rock might have split in the wrong direction, ruining all their previous hard work. The block was then levered out of the way and work started on the next block of stone.

Such work was backbreaking, tedious, and strenuous, often requiring a worker to chisel away at hard stone in the 110-degree

A QUARRY ROAD REDISCOVERED

There can be no doubt that the hardest part of working on a Giza pyramid was the business of moving the heavy stone blocks from the quarry site to the pyramid site. Dragging these stones—which weighed, at a minimum, two or three tons—required much physical strain and backbreaking labor. In 1987 Thomas Bown, a geologist of the U.S. Geological Survey, discovered the remnants of an ancient quarry road on which such stones were delivered for water transportation. The discovery is an important one because this road, built forty-six hundred years ago, has been identified as the oldest known paved road in the world.

The road, located forty miles southwest of Giza, snakes its way across the desert. Bown found the road while working in the Egyptian desert on a project totally unrelated to the pyramids or any ancient quarrying. Portions of the road have been known since 1905, but they had never been identified as a road of ancient origins. In 1993 Bown returned to Egypt for another look at his discovery. He took with him James Harrell, a geologist from the University of Toledo in Ohio. Harrell is an expert on ancient Egyptians and their quarries. Both Bown and Harrell soon discovered the remnants of an ancient basalt quarry. Basalt was not used in the Giza Pyramids themselves, but it had been used for the floor of a mortuary temple at Giza. The two

heat of an Egyptian spring or summer. Quarrymen found working with limestone to be much easier than granite, however, because granite is a much harder stone.

Since it is a harder stone, the Egyptians' tools probably were not as effective. Some experts doubt whether the copper tools in use at the time could have cut through granite. Perhaps the workers rubbed balls of dolerite against the granite, causing it to flake and eventually cut through the rock. Dolerite is an extremely hard, round, green stone found along the banks of the Red Sea. This process would have taken a long time to produce any real amounts of granite blocks for pyramid use. Perhaps this is why granite was used so infrequently in most pyramids. Granite was used for Khufu's sarcophagus, for lining the burial chamber, and as part of the final casing of the pyra-

men discovered pottery fragments in a quarrymen's camp nearby that were dated to the Old Kingdom. Further investigations at the basalt quarry resulted in a microscopic comparison of the basalt found there and the basalt used at Giza, as well as that found at the pyramid sites at Sakkara. These comparisons confirm this quarry to be the source for both sites.

With such evidence in hand, Bown and Harrell completed a study of the road itself. When in use originally, the road led from the quarry to a lake that was connected to the Nile River. The basalt blocks were quarried, then dragged over the paved road to the lake, which has since dried up, causing the road today to lead nowhere. Bown and Harrell speculate that the road was paved because the route to the lake was an uphill trek. Dragging a sledge across the sandy flats and uphill, as well, may well have created a task that the quarry gangs found too difficult to complete without a proper, solid roadbed in place.

The ancient Egyptians paved their road with whatever stone was available. The stone found in the bed includes sandstone, limestone, basalt, and, over a short stretch, petrified wood. Apparently, the road was built to a consistent width, as well—a little less than seven feet, the equivalent of four ancient Egyptian cubits.

mids. But limestone provided the bulk of the millions of stones needed for the three Pyramids of Giza.

Transporting the Stone

Once the limestone or granite blocks were quarried, they were ready for transport. Most of the stones for the Giza Pyramids came from quarries near the pyramid sites, while the granite came from hundreds of miles to the south at Assuan, or Aswan. Recent archaeology has revealed large basin quarries along the edges of the Giza Plateau.

Writer Evan Hadingham describes what archaeologists have discovered at these Giza quarry sites:

Wherever the archaeologists have cleared debris from the bottom of these quarries, one can still see scars in the rock face made by the blows of ancient copper and stone tools. Also visible are huge rectangular slots left behind in the bedrock, where pyramid blocks were prised [pried] out of position, probably with the aid of wooden wedges. From here the blocks were dragged no more than about 500 yards to the pyramid site. Most experts agree that this was the source for the building material.

Much of the better limestone used at Giza came from the Tura quarries, located just across the river from Giza, nestled in the Arabian hills near Cairo. The stones were transported to Giza by boat. Much of it was probably shipped during the flooding season, when the Nile is at its highest. This way the stones could be taken as close to the work site as possible. For the common workers the most difficult part of this process was moving the stones from the Nile to the pyramid site itself.

Moving the stones required two types of boats. One was a large, flat-bottomed barge used to carry some of the larger stones, statues, and obelisks for the pyramid site. The second variety was a smaller craft, canoe shaped, which was used as the basic workhorse of the Nile transportation system. Both kinds of boats were rigged with sails, and both featured two sets of oars to row the boats upstream. Aboard each was a foreman or overseer who managed the loading, shipping, and unloading of his boat. Historian John Weeks describes the scene:

A sailor would beat out the time to a monotonous rhythm. They [the oarsmen] would row in time to this rhythm and probably chant out well-known songs at the same time. This helped them to put up with the hard, back-breaking work of rowing under the hot Egyptian sun. A foreman or overseer would be watching the rowers to see that they did not slack in their work. The man at the helm had a job which required both skill and knowledge of the river. If he made a mistake that boat could easily run aground on one of the many sandbanks in the Nile.

Getting the stones from the quarry to the river and from the river to the pyramid sites presented another challenge. The ancient Egyptians had no practical knowledge of the wheel. They had to haul the cut stones on large sledges, or sleds. These sleds were pushed and pulled by men using ropes. The number of workers needed for each sled varied according to the weight of each stone. Moving this immense deadweight was backbreaking labor. To aid the process, water, or perhaps oil, was poured in front of each sled to make its movements smoother. Even though oxen were available for such difficult

A 1904 photograph reveals the inside of one of the quarry chambers near Giza used during the creation of the Great Pyramid.

TOOLS OF PYRAMID BUILDING

The kinds of tools used on the ancient Egyptian work site were limited and certainly, by modern standards, unsophisticated. Not only did the Egyptians have no practical use of the wheel, they did not have knowledge of something as basic as pulleys. Yet the pyramids stand today, a testimonial to Egyptian skill, determination, and, for them, the right tools. What were these tools used to create the Pyramids of Giza?

Cutting stone was perhaps the task that required the most tools. The Egyptians had use of a variety of tools made from copper or dolerite, a stone substance harder than granite. Saws were in use, also made of copper, but they were pull saws, with the teeth pointing toward the saw handle. (Most modern saws are push saws, with teeth facing away from the handle.) Since copper is a relatively soft metal, such saws and chisels became dull and blunted quickly. Archaeologist and writer John Romer, in his book *Ancient Lives*, describes the use of such tools by limestone quarrymen:

> The quarrymen worked the rock in stepped excavations with copper chisels, discarded one after another as their shanks first tempered, then split with fatigue, or their soft points bent on the flints that ran in straight

a. plumb rule; b. level; c. square; d. trowel; e. mallet

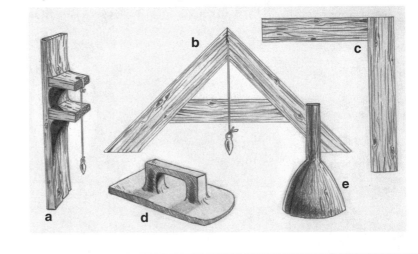

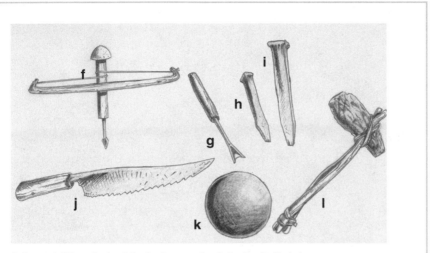

f. bow drill; g. h. i. chisels; j. saw; k. dolerite ball; l. hammer

seams through the cliffs. There was a constant industry concerned with keeping the quarrymen and sculptors . . . in sharpened chisels. Coppersmiths resmelted the worn tools, then beat them into their final shapes by hand: single-pointed spikes for the quarrymen and a wide range of smaller flat-tipped wooden-handled chisels for the sculptors.

Other tools used by the ancient tomb builders included mallets, wedges, and wooden, as well as stone, hammers, each necessary for building a pyramid. Surveyors also used plumb lines and levels. These showed a builder whether a vertical line was straight or not and also whether the top of a stone or a wall was level. Workers used dolerite balls to chip away at both limestone and granite and used stone polishers to put a smooth surface on a stone. Still other tools included trowels and crude drills, whose shafts were turned by hand using a bow string wrapped around them, with the worker moving the bow back and forth. Such tools were crude but very effective. However, most of the work done in the quarries, on the transport boats, and at the pyramid work sites came from one source: the backbreaking labor and muscle of hardworking men.

Erecting the pyramids might have looked something like this. Because hauling stones required concentrated manpower, workers teamed up to drag the stones into position.

work, they were rarely used. Ancient Egyptians felt there were plenty of human workers on hand for such a task, and oxen were considered too valuable for this type of job.

These workers operated in groups called gangs. Seemingly these work groups often competed with one another to see which one could accomplish the most work. Gangs even had nicknames. At the Tura quarries, for example, the men painted the names of their gangs in red ochre on the stones they quarried. These names are still legible on several stones. On the casing blocks at the Medum pyramid, the following are inscribed: Stepped Pyramid Gang, North Gang, Scepter Gang, Vigorous Gang, Enduring Gang, and Boat Gang. Blocks found at the Great Pyramid of Giza bear the name Craftsmen Gang. Why gangs signed their names to these stones is not known. Perhaps it was a way of keeping track of the work accomplished by each gang.

MOVING THE STONES ALONG THE CAUSEWAY

When a boatload of stones arrived at the work site, they were unloaded and prepared for transport up to the pyramid site. Once on site, many of the stones were cut further to prepare them for their specific position in the pyramid. A causeway or road connected the pyramid site to the Nile so the stones could be moved. Eventually walls were constructed along the causeway and a roof added for later use as the route for delivery of the pharaoh's body to its final resting place. Such a causeway made the transporting of stones to the pyramid site much easier than it had been to carry them from a quarry site to a Nile barge in the first place. With the moving of stones onto the pyramid site, all was ready for the construction of the Pyramids of Giza.

FIRST STAGES OF
CONSTRUCTION

The Pyramids of Giza still hold many mysteries for modern historians, archaeologists, and Egyptologists. The tombs stand as monuments to the ingenuity of the ancient Egyptians, a people who lacked, by today's standards, any sophisticated equipment in building the Giza Pyramids. For the past two hundred years the experts have examined the evidence, however, and produced several noteworthy conclusions for the most often asked questions concerning these forty-five-hundred-year-old architectural wonders. These questions center around such mysteries as how many people were needed to build these monuments, what construction techniques they used, and how the purposes of the pyramids determined how they were built, both inside and outside.

Evan Hadingham, writing about the pyramids in the *Atlantic,* writes about the continuing search for clues to the most often asked questions concerning the pyramids:

> [The] evidence of high precision, which has provoked many farfetched theories, including the use of prehistoric lasers and extraterrestrial architects, continues to perplex even the most level-headed researchers. Without dump trucks and jackhammers, how did the Egyptians ever manage to assemble the Great Pyramid's towering pile of 2.5 million limestone blocks? Without modern surveying instruments, how could they have controlled its shape so accurately, particularly the even 52 degrees slope of its smooth outer casing? And how could the construction job have been accomplished in just twenty-three years, the time span allotted to Khufu's reign . . . ? Given a ten-hour working day and a year-round building program that works out to one block set in place every two minutes!

While such questions are still being asked, archaeologists today are reducing their theories to a handful of choices. Over the past ten years new evidence has been unearthed at Giza, and new theories of construction have gained support that begin to unlock the mysteries that have clouded the building of the Giza monuments.

TYPES OF WORKERS

Archaeologists are in general agreement that Egyptian peasant farmers provided the majority of the unskilled workforce for building the Pyramids of Giza. Such workers lived near the pyramid site in worker villages, which might be largely abandoned during the agricultural season. Archaeologists have uncovered such a village or barracks complex capable of housing four thousand workers near the Great Pyramid. These workers were divided into work gangs made up of anywhere from eight to twenty-five men. Each gang had one foreman, probably a soldier. Such workers were usually not paid wages, but instead received food and clothing for their labor.

In addition to the need for unskilled laborers, the work at Giza required the efforts of skilled workmen as well. Surveyors helped find suitable sites for the pyramids. Scribes were needed to tally expenditures, keep tabs on workers and their assignments, and inventory supplies and other records. Then came the overseers, who organized the work at the quarries that produced the stones. They monitored the work of the bargers, masons, and the men who moved the stones onto the work site and into place.

PYRAMID AND QUARRY SITES

Mediterranean Sea
DELTA
Giza • Modern Cairo
Sakkara • Tura Limestone Quarry
Dashur •
Medum •
Gulf of Suez
Nile River
Assuan Granite Quarry

PLANNING AHEAD

Before pyramid workers dragged the first layer of stones into place on the monument site, they began to carve their way into the solid bedrock. Each of the three Giza Pyramids has at least

one underground passage. Workers began work on these passages and chambers, probably while the pyramid site was being leveled and measured. Using dolerite balls, workers ground away at the bedrock, creating their subterranean chambers. Other workers completed the chambers with chisels, smoothing out the rock walls. Once a burial chamber was completed, the sarcophagus, or stone coffin, for the pharaoh was brought on the site and placed in the chamber.

Once the rooms and passageways beneath the pyramid were finished, construction of the rooms and corridors inside the super-structure began. Historian John Weeks describes the process of creating rooms in the interior:

A supervisor looks on as workers use a wooden lever to hoist a massive stone into place.

The rooms and corridors of the pyramid itself had to be put in whilst the pyramid was being built. The stones used were usually best quality limestone, granite and other hard rocks. The builders decided on which level they wanted a room and what its size was going to be. The stones were then probably cut to size on the ground, and often put together and numbered before being sent up the pyramid. There they would be very carefully put together again, rather like a jigsaw puzzle, using the numbers as a check. The squares or layers would be built up around the rooms and corridors. The corridors and rooms had to be well built because thousands of tons of stone would be resting on their roofs.

PAINTING THE PYRAMIDS RED

The Giza Pyramids were originally covered with white Tura limestone blocks, which gave them a glimmering appearance as they reflected the rays of a bright desert sun. However, according to chemical tests made on fragments of casing stones from the Great Pyramid and the pyramid of Khafre, it is possible that portions of the Giza Pyramids were also painted. These chemical tests show elements that are not naturally found in such stones. One chemist claimed that the pyramids were "coated with a thin layer of siliceous [containing silica or sand] gypsum plaster and painted with a pigment of red ochre."

Remnants of pyramid casing stones do not appear white today. They have shades of color from ochre, or brownish red, to gray. However, not all the experts agree that these colors are due to any painting done by humans. Probably, they argue, these color variations are due to weathering.

In looking for an answer to this question of color, an additional piece of evidence plays an important role. Hieroglyphics that date from the Old Kingdom show pictures of white pyramids with a reddish stripe around their bases and a capstone of yellow or blue. In such pictographs the red suggests pink granite, which was used on the base of the Khafre pyramid. In addition, the blue could represent gray granite. The yellow is often assumed to symbolize gold, for there is some evidence that pyramid capstones were sometimes overlaid in gold. Given these colors,

Ancient pictographs showing red, yellow, and blue pyramids suggest that the Giza pyramids might also have been colorfully painted.

those who doubt that the pyramids were painted argue that if they were actually painted, such hieroglyphics would show them as red, rather than white, the color of Tura limestone.

A sketch of the sarcophagus found in the elaborate and complex interior of Khufu's pyramid.

Some pyramid experts theorize that construction of internal elements of these monuments, such as shafts, tunnels, and burial chambers, took place nearly independent of the external work of the pyramid. Since corridors and chambers took up such a small amount of space inside a pyramid—especially the Khafre and Menkaure monuments—separate work crews could have busied themselves with these internal spaces while other work gangs labored on the pyramid's exterior. Archaeologists speculate that work on internal passageways and burial chambers might have progressed at a faster rate vertically than the pyramid's outside construction.

BENEATH KHAFRE'S PYRAMID

Such subterranean shafts and chambers were used on all three Giza Pyramids. In two of these pyramids—those of Khafre and Menkaure—such underground tunnels and burial chambers make up their only internal rooms. The third pyramid, the Great Pyramid of Khufu, is more elaborate inside. Its interior features subterranean shafts and an unfinished chamber located deep in the bedrock beneath the pyramid structure, but its actual burial chamber is located inside the pyramid structure's center. This fact makes the pyramid of Khufu not only the largest of the three, but the most complex inside.

Khafre's pyramid has two known entrances, both on the northern face. One is found about fifty feet up the northern side. The other was carved in the rock foundation on which the pyramid rests. The upper passageway enters the pyramid at a twenty-five-degree angle and cuts through the pyramid until it hits the rockbed. Once under the pyramid, the tunnel becomes horizontal, extending on until it reaches about halfway across the base of the pyramid. There lies the tomb chamber. All these—the tunnel, passageway, and tomb—are lined with red granite. The chamber measures over forty-six feet in length, over sixteen feet in width, and over twenty-two feet in height. Here sits the pharaoh's sarcophagus, made of polished granite. Its lid was removed sometime in the past and broken into two pieces, which are still on the chamber floor. The chamber was found in this condition in 1818 when a European pyramid explorer named Giovanni Belzoni entered Khafre's tomb. Belzoni found no trace of Khafre's mummified remains. The upper passageway and vault were intended for the burial of Khafre's body. But what was the purpose of the second shaft below? That outer shaft slopes down underneath the pyramid at a twenty-one-degree angle and then also turns horizontally into a wider chamber measuring thirty-four feet in length, ten feet across, and eight feet five inches in height. Archaeologists remain unsure of its purpose.

Some believe it was a mistake. Egyptologists theorize that when the outer tunnel and chamber were built, the plans were to construct the pyramid farther north by approximately two hundred feet. This would have placed the chamber directly under the apex, or center, of the pyramid. Possibly the plans changed after the tunnel and vault were built, when a better rock foundation was discovered slightly to the south. Other than these two passageways and chambers underground, the pyramid of Khafre is a solid mass of stone, much like its neighbor, Menkaure's pyramid.

BENEATH MENKAURE'S PYRAMID

The smallish pyramid of Menkaure covers only one-fourth the area of its neighbor to the northeast. Its vertical height stands today at 204 feet, 14 feet off its original height. Its passageways

THE SPHINX: MONUMENT WITH A FACE

Crouching on the desert horizon near the Great Pyramid of Khufu, a strange animal stares out across the desert. It is the Great Sphinx, and it looks like no animal ever seen before. The giant statue is made of stone and features the head of a man and the body of a lion. Who built this peculiar creature and why?

The Great Sphinx was built at the same time as the Giza Pyramids. Archaeologists are fairly certain that the statue was built during the reign of Khafre. The body and head were carved from a single knoll of limestone that was left exposed after workers finished quarrying stone for the Great Pyramid. Its size is enormous. The Sphinx measures 240 feet in length and stands 66 feet tall. At its widest point, the face measures 13 feet 8 inches. The lion's feet, which extend out from the statue's base, are made of brick.

The name sphinx was given to the statue by the Greeks. Their myths include an imaginary creature by that name that usually had a human head, a lion's body, a serpent's tail, and wings. The Great Sphinx has no tail or wings, however. The Great Sphinx is not the only statue of its kind in Egypt, but it is the largest. Others resemble the Great Sphinx with its human head, yet some have the heads of other animals, such as rams and hawks. Near the Great Temple of Amon-Re at Karnak, in southern Egypt, ram-headed sphinxes line the main avenue.

The face of the Great Sphinx may be that of a pharaoh, perhaps Khafre; or that of an Egyptian god, perhaps Harmakhis, a human representation of the sun god; or Horus, the god who guarded temples and sacred shrines.

In fact, the last representation might explain the purpose of the Great Sphinx. Some historians believe the Sphinx was constructed to serve as a guardian for the Giza Pyramids. In Egyptian mythology the lion is often portrayed as the keeper and guardian of sacred places. The lion is also thought to be the guardian of the underworld gates. An inscription found near one sphinx in Egypt recognizes this purpose:

> I protect the chapel of thy tomb. I guard the sepulchral [burial] chamber. I ward off the intruding stranger. I hurl the foes to the ground and their weapons with them. I drive away the wicked one from the chapel of

thy tomb. I destroy thine adversaries in their lurking-place, blocking it that they come forth no more.

Since it was carved and constructed, the Great Sphinx has had its share of problems. From time to time invading armies, such as the Turks and the French under Napoleon Bonaparte, have used the Sphinx for target practice. In addition, the shifting sands of the Egyptian desert have repeatedly covered up the statue, nearly to its neck. An ancient story is told about a young Egyptian prince named Thutmose, who lived during the 1400s B.C. One day, while hunting, Thutmose rested in the shadow of the Great Sphinx. While the prince slept, the Sphinx spoke to him, begging him to remove the sand that covered its paws. In return, the Sphinx promised to make Thutmose pharaoh of Egypt. Thutmose did as the Sphinx asked and later became Thutmose IV. Sand has been cleared from the Sphinx several times since the days of the Roman Empire and more recently in 1818, 1886, and 1925–1926.

Some historians believe that Egyptians created the imposing stone statue the Great Sphinx to guard the Pyramids of Giza.

and chambers are largely located beneath the pyramid structure itself, as with the Khafre pyramid. These tunnels probably reflect a design change made while the pyramid was being built. The original down-sloping tunnel runs under the pyramid and becomes horizontal as it opens into a burial chamber. All this is typical in construction except for one feature: The opening of the tunnel never reaches the outer wall of the pyramid, but rather ends abruptly at ground level, representing a tunnel that leads nowhere.

Archaeologists have developed a theory that may explain the tunnel's existence. The solution may lie in a second tunnel and a probable design change in the pyramid. The second tunnel, sloped at approximately the same angle as the first, may be entered from the pyramid's north wall. This shaft runs to a horizontal passageway, which itself extends just under the horizontal tunnel connecting to the original sloped shaft. The experts theorize that the reason for two shafts is that the pyramid of Menkaure was enlarged at a later date from its original design. Under the original design, the first tunnel would have had an outside entrance. The extended design made that first tunnel a dead end.

Both of these tunnels open into a larger chamber directly under the pyramid's apex, or interior center. Beneath this chamber another horizontal passageway has been discovered, running west, or perpendicular to the two original passageways. This final tunnel leads to a second chamber. This chamber once served as the pharaoh's burial chamber. Today, it stands empty. The sarcophagus was removed by archaeologist Colonel Richard Howard-Vyse during an expedition in 1837 and 1838. This sarcophagus was made of basalt, a hard, dark-colored rock.

BEGINNING CONSTRUCTION

Although the three large pyramids at Giza differ in size and in their interior room and passageway structure, they were all constructed following the same basic building pattern. Once each pyramid site had been properly and accurately leveled, the first layer of stones was hauled to the site, and actual construction began on the pyramid itself. Soon the burial chamber was covered over with stones. The underground shafts extended into the interior of the pyramid itself until the angled shaft reached an exterior wall. This opening would serve as the entrance to the pyramid's burial chamber once the structure was completed.

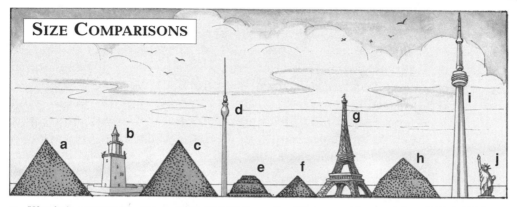

a. Khufu's pyramid, Giza 480 ft/146.5 m; b. Pharos, Alexandria, 590 ft/180 m;
c. Khafre's pyramid, Giza 470 ft/143.5 m; d. Television Tower, Berlin 1198 ft/365 m; e.
Step Pyramid, Sakkara 197 ft/60 m; f. Menkaure's pyramid, Giza 218 ft/66.5 m;
g. Eiffel Tower, Paris 1043 ft/318 m; h. Bent Pyramid, Dahshur 320 ft/97 m; i. CN Tower,
Toronto 1820 ft/555 m; j. Statue of Liberty, New York 305 ft/93 m

Without the use of pulleys, the ancient Egyptians pulled
the great stones on sledges to the center of the pyramid base.
The stones were placed in the base to form the shape of a
square. These core stones or blocks were cut fairly roughly.
Core stones were used to form the pyramid's interior and were
never intended to be seen. Once the workers had laid stones to
the outer edge of the pyramid, they stopped using core stones.
They then moved on to packing blocks.

Packing blocks were cut much more precisely. These stones
made up the next to the last row of stones. Since the casing
blocks, or outer layer of stones, were laid against them, the
packing blocks had to be cut just right. Once these stones were
in place, the workers had basically finished the inside of the
pyramid.

Finally came the casing blocks. These stones were all-
important, for they were the ones that showed. Only the best
quality limestone, that quarried at Tura, was used for such important blocks. Unlike nearly all the interior blocks, casing
blocks were not cut squarish, but rather with a sloping side,
much like a prism, or a three-dimensional triangle. The slope
gave the pyramid its outer angle. Before each casing stone was
put into place, masons spread a layer of mortar on the packing
stones. The casing stones were sledged and levered into place,
and the mortar cushioned their position, making a tight fit for
each outer stone.

Not all archaeologists agree that the pyramids were built from the inside out, with workers laying the core blocks, followed by packing stones and finally the casing blocks. English Egyptologist Sir Flinders Petrie, who directed archaeological excavations at Giza from 1880 to 1914, became convinced, based on his study of the Great Pyramid, that the outer casing stones were placed first, and the interior stones laid afterwards. Each casing stone came to its resting place on the pyramid fully dressed and smoothed and was then cemented into position. After the casing stones on a given level were put in place, Petrie suggested that the workers filled in the layer with packing stones and the core blocks. With this theory, the outer face of each casing block was smoothed individually before being placed on the pyramid's exterior. To support his position, Petrie offered the following evidence: "There is a small difference of

In contrast to most archaeologists, who believed that the pyramids were built from the inside out, English Egyptologist Sir Flinders Petrie theorized that Egyptians laid the casing blocks, or outside layer of stones, first and the interior stones afterwards.

MYSTERIOUS TOMB

Deep under the Menkaure pyramid, archaeologist Colonel Richard Howard-Vyse, during an expedition in 1837 and 1838, found
not only a rectangular, basalt sarcophagus,
but he also discovered bones resting under
a wooden coffin lid, which bore the name
Menkaure.

However, it is here that a great mystery
begins. Twentieth-century radiocarbon test-
ing, designed to date the age of such bones,
has shown that they were not nearly old
enough to be Menkaure's corpse by several
thousand years. Someone, for unknown reasons, had tampered with the original remains
sometime in the past. In fact, the bones that
Howard-Vyse discovered have been dated to
less than two thousand years ago.

Today the wooden lid and the mummified bones found in the crypt rest in the
British Museum. Unfortunately, the basalt
sarcophagus cannot be seen today, for it
was lost at sea when the ship carrying it to
England capsized off the Spanish coast,
sending the ancient coffin to the ocean
floor.

Lid of Menkaure's
coffin.

angle between the [casing] blocks at their junction, proving
that the faces have not been even smoothed since being built
together." Petrie's point is that if the casing stones had been
mortared in place as the last step after construction of the su-
perstructure was finished, the exposed face of the casing
stones would have been laid at exactly the same angle to one
another.

Once the casing stones were in place, the work on the
pyramid's first layer was complete. But every other layer after
this one had one special problem. For all other layers, not only
did the workers have to move the stones into place, but they
also had to move them *up*, with two results. First, building the
pyramid higher and higher required the construction of ramps

to deliver the building materials to each level and second, with the addition of each level, the work space on the pyramid grew smaller and smaller.

NUMBER OF WORKERS

With construction projects as large as the Giza Pyramids, two questions are often asked: How many years did it take to build each pyramid, and how many workers were required? The answers to these two questions are not easy ones. The Greek historian Herodotus, writing two thousand years after the Giza Pyramids were constructed, claimed that the Great Pyramid of Khufu was built in twenty years. As to the number of workers, Herodotus writes that the Great Pyramid was built by four hundred thousand men, each for a "period of three months." That means that one hundred thousand workers were at work on the Great Pyramid during every month of each year. However, many Egyptologists believe that work on the pyramids took place only during the three-month period each year when the Nile River was at its highest stages. These were the months when the fields could not be worked, freeing up farmers for pyramid construction, and when transporting stones was easiest.

Among archaeologists who are refining ideas about how the pyramids were built is Professor Mark Lehner of the University of Chicago. He has been studying the Giza site since the early 1980s. Lehner believes that construction of the pyramids at Giza required as few as ten thousand workers. In 1991 he and a team of experts, including local stonemasons, experimented with building a minipyramid using blocks of Tura limestone. *National Geographic* writer David Roberts describes Lehner's project:

> To gauge the extent of . . . labor [required to build a Giza pyramid], Mark Lehner and a team built a 30-foot-high pyramid near Giza. . . . Using a helical ramp winding upward around their pyramid, Lehner's team found that just ten to twelve men could slide a block up the ramp, using desert clay and water as a lubricant, and lever it into place. Herodotus declared that 100,000 men were needed to build one of the Pyramids at Giza. Lehner calculates that as few as 10,000 could have pulled off the job.

Experimental field research such as Lehner's has helped him and other archaeologists gain a clearer picture in estimating how many workers were needed to build the monuments at Giza.

While modern archaeology has managed to shed much light on the logistics of how and why the Egyptian pyramids were built, much work remains to be done. As these highly trained experts sift through the remnants of construction scattered across the Giza Plateau, theories come and go, replaced by new interpretations and fresh evidence. Yet despite the various modern explanations concerning how the pyramids were built, the experts still all agree on one thing: Construction of the pyramids at Giza was a monumental task requiring exacting detail work, thousands of workers exerting themselves to Herculean efforts, and an extraordinary dedication of the people of that ancient land.

Final Stages of Construction

After two hundred years of archaeological examination of the ancient pyramids of Egypt, major questions still remain unanswered. The one that receives, perhaps, the greatest attention from archaeologists and Egyptologists centers on the construction techniques used to build the pyramids. How did the Egyptians, with their simple technologies and their lack of the wheel and pulley, manage to haul huge blocks of limestone to such heights and place them with such precision? Since the nineteenth century scholars have repeatedly speculated on this subject. Today the logical answers to this complex question, those answers that the experts take seriously, have been reduced to just a few. Basically, they hinge on the use of ramps that gave the Egyptian workers a platform on which to drag their building blocks up higher and higher as the pyramid grew vertically.

In *The Pyramids of Egypt*, historian and Egyptologist I. E. S. Edwards explains the need and purpose for such ramps in pyramid construction:

> In the absence of the pulley—a device which does not seem to have been known in Egypt before Roman times—only one method of raising heavy weights was open to the ancient Egyptians, namely by means of ramps composed of brick and earth which sloped upwards from the level of the ground to whatever height was desired. . . . Finally, when the wall had been built to its full height, the ramp would be dismantled and the outer faces of the stones, which had not previously been made smooth, dressed course by course downwards as the level of the ramp was reduced.

THE EASTERN SUPPLY RAMP THEORY

One widely accepted theory, known as the eastern supply ramp theory, suggests that a supply ramp was built on the pyramid's east side, since it was closest to the Nile, where boats delivered their stone block cargoes. Such a ramp would have been made of earth, rubble, and mud bricks. It would have required a slight grade or angle so that it would not be too steep for pushing and pulling block-laden sledges. Naturally, the steeper the grade or incline, the more difficult the task of sliding two-ton blocks of limestone up the ramp. Some experts suggest that such a supply ramp might have risen one foot higher for every twelve feet of length.

Evidence of such ramps being used in monument construction in ancient Egypt does exist. For example, an Egyptian document written on papyrus and now located in the British Museum gives approximate measurements for a proposed ramp to be used in temple construction during Egypt's Twelfth Dynasty (1320–1200 B.C.). While not the same time frame as that of the pyramid building at Giza, the basic idea could have easily dated from the days of the Old Kingdom. The ramp described in this ancient papyrus measured 415 yards in length, was 32 yards in width, and had a height of 35 yards. This works out to a grade for the ramp of 1 to 12; in other words, a ramp that extended 12 feet in length for every 1 foot rise in height. A stone ramp built for the mortuary temple of Menkaure, which still exists today, has a grade of 1 to 8. The grade of a ramp probably depended on the weight of the materials being delivered on it.

Since such ramps rose as the pyramid height grew, the length of the ramp became longer and longer. This was the only way to keep the steepness of the ramp consistent during construction. For example, if the pyramid's first layer of stone was 5 feet high, the supply ramp was extended out from the pyramid a distance of 60 feet. By comparison, when the pyramid reached a height of, say, 50 feet, the ramp was extended out to a length of 600 feet. Even when construction on the pyramid was completed and its capstone firmly in place, the supply ramps were not immediately torn down. The workers then began the long process of cleaning and polishing the pyramid's outer casing stones. Ramps were taken down only as workers completed the finish work on the pyramid's exterior surfaces.

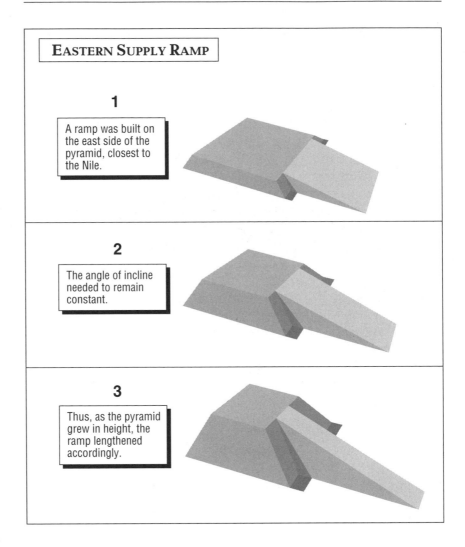

EASTERN SUPPLY RAMP

1

A ramp was built on the east side of the pyramid, closest to the Nile.

2

The angle of incline needed to remain constant.

3

Thus, as the pyramid grew in height, the ramp lengthened accordingly.

THEORY PROBLEMS

While some scholars and archaeologists hold to the single-ramp theory, others seriously question it. Those experts cite the facts that make such a theory highly suspect. For example, such a ramp had to be built as the pyramid rose from the desert floor, causing its length to extend horizontally at the same time. A single ramp that rose to the height of the Great Pyramid of Khufu would have been nearly five hundred feet high. If the ramp extended out horizontally based on a grade of one to twelve, the resulting ramp would have extended a distance of over one mile. This, according to some scholars, is difficult to imagine.

Writer Evan Hadingham presents a logical argument against the use of a single building ramp in constructing the Giza Pyramids:

> Even if dragging stones up a mile-long ramp had been practical, constructing it would have been a monumental engineering challenge. A quick calculation shows that a ramp of this size would have required at least three times as much building material as the pyramid itself. In any case, since the quarry and the pyramid were only about 500 yards apart, a mile-long ramp would not have been useful.

THE FOUR-RAMP THEORY

Another ramp theory has the ancient builders beginning one ramp at each corner of the pyramid. Such ramps did not extend to great lengths out from the pyramid as required with an east-side supply ramp. Instead, they moved up each side, like a snake coiling around the monument, rising higher and higher. In 1950 engineers at the Museum of Science in Boston, Massachusetts, built a scale model of a pyramid under construction using just such a ramp design. With the miniature model, the four-ramp theory, also known as the coiling-ramp theory, did not reveal any problems that might have hampered the ancient Egyptian workers in constructing the Giza monuments.

In addition, archaeologists have recently begun to theorize that such a series of ramps was not constructed from simply mud brick, which probably could not bear the weight of five-thousand-pound stone blocks, but instead were built of *tafla*.

Tafla is a local clay that is still mined in Egypt today and used as a multipurpose mortar in modern stone building construction. Recent discoveries at the Giza site point to the possible use of *tafla* in building the Giza monuments. Archaeologist Mark Lehner has unearthed the remains of ancient *tafla* ramps on the Giza Plateau, one of which stands at a height of ten feet. *Tafla* may represent the secret ingredient in ancient Egyptian ramp building. It is a material that bonds well with rock, creating a mass that is stronger than mud brick, yet lighter in weight. Not only would *tafla*-based ramps be lightweight, compared to ones constructed from mud brick, it could be more easily broken up, as one expert claims "with a few swings of a pick."

A ROYAL TOMB ROBBER

Since tomb robbers are technically thieves, they are usually not known to us by name. They did their work in secret, greedily risking their lives for gold and jewels. However, history can put a name on one pyramid robber.

Al-Mamun, who lived from A.D. 786 to 833, was a young caliph, or ruler from the ancient Islamic city of Baghdad. His father, Harun ar-Rashid, is usually thought to be the caliph mentioned in the collection of tales called *The Arabian Nights*. Found in the pages of one of those stories is a legend about the Great Pyramid of Khufu. The legend says that great riches lay buried in the immense Egyptian tomb. But the story also tells of great knowledge sealed inside the pyramid. Books and texts and maps, including a chart of the heavens, could be found in the Great Pyramid. After reading the legend, al-Mamun was intrigued. He was a philosopher and scientist, and the story of an ancient repository of great knowledge appealed to him as much as the lure of gold and wealth.

To find for himself what lay within the walls of the Great Pyramid, al-Mamun mounted an expedition of scientists, architects, engineers, and workers and made the trip across the Arabian desert to the land of the pharaohs.

Everyone on the expedition was excited when they arrived at Giza and took their first looks at the Pyramids. The monuments were like nothing they had ever seen before. Immediately they set to work, under al-Mamun's direction,

It is possible that both types of ramps were used in constructing pyramids in ancient Egypt. The single ramp would have been more feasible for a smaller pyramid, such as those built near the Pyramids of Giza for the pharaohs' queens and family members. The coil design might lend itself to use on the giant monuments of Khufu, Khafre, and Menkaure.

MOVING THE STONES UPWARD

Regardless of which type of ramp was used in building the pyramids, experts theorize that wooden logs were laid down side by side, and pyramid stones were moved over the surface of these logs, lubricated by water or oil poured over them.

to find their way into the Great Pyramid. Legend told of a secret entrance, a door that allowed one to follow a secret passage deep inside the pyramid, leading to its treasures. For weeks, al-Mamun's men searched, but no entrance could be found.

Frustrated, the young prince ordered his workers to create their own door. The men went to work on the massive stones, hammering away with their chisels and battering rams. They arranged fires, which heated the outer stones. Then cold vinegar was thrown on the hot stones, cracking them. After several more weeks, the workers broke through, discovering a passage. Unfortunately for them, this passage did not produce the pharaoh's tomb or its riches. Months passed before al-Mamun's men discovered another passage that led to the

Seeking jewels and other treasure, al-Mamun expresses disappointment at finding an empty tomb.

Grand Gallery and ultimately to the burial chamber of Khufu. But when they entered the chamber and opened the great stone sarcophagus, it was as empty as the chamber itself. Al-Mamun found no treasure, no pharaoh, and no ancient wisdom. What happened to the treasures of Khufu's tomb and the mummy of the pharaoh remains a mystery.

If a single ramp was used, the mound and its wooden logs were probably placed around the entire pyramid. This further aided in moving stones more specifically into place. A platform that was built on the other three sides of the pyramid projected out enough distance—perhaps thirty or forty feet—so that the workers could perform their tasks. According to this theory the platform gave the workers foothold embankments to work on. It also means that as the ramp and its embankments were built up, they covered the pyramid from sight, temporarily burying the project as it rose from the desert floor.

Tafla may have been the answer for another problem of the pyramid builders. Since this work depended on the sheer muscle power of hundreds and even thousands of workers, modern experts wonder how workers could have hauled the two- or three-ton blocks of limestone up the construction ramps by hand without collapsing from exhaustion. The common theory that the work gangs used wooden rollers to slide their limestone blocks over and up the ramp is one not as readily accepted as it has been in the past. Modern experiments with this type of structure have shown that such a procedure would have been slow going and backbreaking.

The construction of the massive pyramids was an incredible technical feat. Pictured is an artist's conception of Egyptians putting stones in place using a series of ropes and logs.

However, experiments have shown how much easier the work would have been if ramps had been built using wooden planks laid down like railroad tracks and coated with a layer of wet *tafla*. Archaeologist Mark Lehner describes an experiment his team carried out, using this technique:

> We were trying to move the sled on rollers up the trackway, and had twenty men hauling away on the ropes, slipping and sweating, and we were getting nowhere. So we had a new idea—forget about the rollers and try simply sliding the sleds up the wet wood of the trackway. The masons protested furiously, 'It won't work!' but we said, 'Just give it a try!' They poured water on the wooden planks, eased the sled off the rollers, and next thing we knew it took off like a bar of soap.

CONSTRUCTION UPWARD

The work on the pyramids required the ancient Egyptians to conquer other construction problems. As their work went ever upward, the pyramid engineers had to keep the pyramid's design accurately squared. As they placed layer upon layer of stone, any errors in the angles would result in a less than perfect monument, one that could be twisted just enough so that the four sides under construction would not meet squarely at the pyramid's peak. Just one or two slightly mis-cut stones could result in such a problem. Archaeologists have long wondered how the Egyptians managed to keep the pyramid's sides exactly square to each other, resulting in a consistent ninety-degree angle between each side.

University of Chicago Egyptologist Mark Lehner may have discovered the answer during his Giza investigations, which took place in the late 1980s and early 1990s. For decades archaeologists had observed a series of postholes around the base of the Great Pyramid. No one had ever determined the purpose of those holes. Lehner developed a theory that these holes held wooden posts and that a string or cord was extended from pole to pole, creating a level line around the base of the pyramid. This line could serve as a reference line in reading just how level each layer of stone on the pyramid was before the workers moved on to the next level. The outer edge of each new layer of

DIGGING UP A PHARAOH'S BOAT

In 1954 archaeologists made an important discovery near the Great Pyramid of Khufu. They found a great funeral boat, buried in a stone chamber, hidden by the sands of the Giza desert.

Ancient Egyptians, feeling the need to provide their dead pharaoh with transportation in the afterlife, had buried the wooden boat in a pit measuring 102 feet long, nearly 12 feet deep, and 8½ feet wide. Huge limestone blocks, each weighing 15 tons, had covered the pit for 4,600 years, their joints cemented by thick layers of mortar.

The boat had been stored disassembled in 1,224 pieces. Archaeologists and Egyptologists reassembled the vessel, which measured 142 feet in length. Today the ancient Nile bark, or boat, is housed in a special museum near the Great Pyramid of Khufu.

The archaeologists who unearthed the royal bark were amazed to find, upon opening the pit, that the chamber had been sealed airtight. A *National Geographic* reporter quoted one of those present as saying they smelled "vapors, perfumes of the wood, sacred wood of the ancient religion." The pit had been sealed so thoroughly that the boat's cedar timbers and their scent were preserved inside the desert storage vault for centuries.

During excavations in the boat vault, archaeologists found evidence of a second pit nearby. However, that chamber was not investigated until 1985 when *National Geographic* magazine sponsored a technological expedition.

stone added to the pyramid's exterior would have run parallel to the observable cord line running along each side.

INSIDE THE GREAT PYRAMID OF KHUFU

As the great stone structures at Giza rose from the desert floor, their interiors also took shape. Of the three pyramids, the Great Pyramid of Khufu probably represented the greatest technical challenge. The pyramids of Khafre and Menkaure are solid masses of stone with all burial chambers, vaults, and tunnels carved underground, probably before the massive stones were even set in place. Khufu's pyramid, on the other hand, contains

Upon investigation, a second boat was, indeed, discovered. This archaeological project did not result in the removal of this second boat, however. The burial pit was broken into by a special drill through the vault's ceiling, creating a hole only three inches in diameter. A specially designed camera was inserted in the hole, which filmed the ship on videotape.

Once the vault was drilled open, sensors were inserted to examine the air. To everyone's disappointment, the air was not ancient. Somehow, the seal on the boat pit had been broken some time in the past. An Egyptologist named Hag Ahmed Yousef, who was on site during the 1954 excavation, and again present at the 1985 project, thought he had an answer. Yousef had directed the construction of the first boat for housing in the new museum. He recalled a brick-making machine and a cement mixer that had been used in the 1960s to construct the boat museum. Both pieces of equipment had been positioned just above the second boat pit. Perhaps the vibrations of the mixer had broken the seal of the ancient burial vault.

The oblong pit near Khufu's pyramid that once housed a funeral boat.

When the camera investigation was completed, the second boat was left in the pit, not to be removed. The drill hole was plugged with an aluminum cork and gypsum mortar. It still lies in its ancient vault, once again undisturbed.

a complex of underground shafts and chambers as well as an elaborate series of tunnels, airshafts, and passageways rising through the pyramid's center. The pharaoh's burial chamber also lies within the raised pyramid structure.

The original entrance to the Great Pyramid was on the north side, about 55 feet up the pyramid's northern slope. Measuring less than 4 feet on each side, a squarish tunnel descends through the pyramid at a 26-degree angle into bedrock. This tunnel goes on for 345 feet, longer than a football field. At that point, the tunnel levels out and continues horizontally for 29 additional feet and ends in a chamber under the Great Pyramid's apex. Measuring 46 feet by 27 feet and 11 feet 6 inches high, this chamber was never finished. Extending out from the south wall of the chamber is a blind tunnel, leading nowhere. Perhaps a second chamber was intended, but one was never built. Experts today do not know why the builders made a change in plans and abandoned this chamber.

Author Desmond Stewart notes this change in construction, one that even modern experts cannot explain:

> Only when the pyramid had advanced by several courses was a second plan made: to construct the chamber in the exact center of the pyramid, but not very high above ground level. It was now too late to plan for a corridor leading straight from the pyramid entrance to the pyramid's heart. Instead, the roof of the descending corridor was pierced and a new ascending corridor . . . was constructed. This culminated, under the second plan, in a horizontal passage leading to the misnamed Queen's chamber, intended for Khufu.

A sketch of the entrance to the narrow tunnel that leads to the internal chambers of the Great Pyramid.

This second tunnel extended 129 feet toward the pyramid's interior at a 26-degree angle. Since the stone layers above the original descending tunnel had already been laid in place, this tunnel ascending from the original required the Egyptian workers to chisel their way through solid limestone. At the end of this carved shaft the tunnel becomes horizontal and proceeds directly to the center of the pyramid to a chamber that has traditionally been called the Queen's Chamber. This chamber measures nearly 19 feet from east to west and over 17 feet from north to south. Its highest point is 20 feet 5 inches. Again, for some unknown reason, this chamber, too, was abandoned and left unfinished.

THE GRAND GALLERY AND BEYOND

Located above the Queen's Chamber, deep inside the Great Pyramid, are the Grand Gallery and the King's Chamber. Both structures are unique among Giza pyramids and reveal an architectural talent that goes beyond the general construction found in most pyramids. That ascending corridor—the offshoot from the original descending tunnel—continues above the level of the Queen's Chamber and opens up into a marvelous corridor. The Grand Gallery is 153 feet in length and reaches 28 feet in height. The gallery walls are of polished limestone. The chamber progressively narrows at several levels up its walls, creating a corbelled vault, so that it is wider at the bottom than at the top. Along both parallel walls of the gallery is a flat-topped ramp measuring 2 feet tall and less than 2 feet in width.

Egyptologist Kurt Mendelssohn describes the purpose of this large corridor in the heart of the Khufu pyramid:

> This impressive high passage, usually called the Grand Gallery, was for a long time believed to have served ritualistic purposes until it was discovered by Flinders Petrie that its real object was to serve as a store for a series of large limestone blocks. These blocks, when the tomb chamber was to be sealed, were let down into the ascending passage where, in fact, three of them are still in position.

At the gallery's far end is a short, narrow passage, about three feet above the gallery floor, exiting directly into the King's Chamber, the burial place of the pharaoh. This large vault measures over thirty-four feet east to west, seventeen feet north to south, and towers to a height of over nineteen feet. Above the burial chamber are five separate chambers, stacked on top of one another. Each has a flat roof, except the upper one, which features a pointed or angled roof. These chambers were probably built to keep the roof from caving in directly on top of the pharaoh's sarcophagus.

The sarcophagus was long ago plundered by tomb robbers. Although the rough, granite box is still in place, its lid and

HEMIUNU: ARCHITECT TO KHUFU

While the architect of the pharaoh Zoser, Grand Vizier Imhotep, is the most remembered and revered of ancient Egypt, another name has survived to receive his rightful credit as a great building designer. His name was Hemiunu. He was a cousin of Khufu and was, therefore, a member of the royal family. Unlike the mysterious Imhotep, about whom modern archaeologists know very little, a likeness of Hemiunu has survived.

The likeness is in the form of a full-size limestone statue. In this form Hemiunu appears to be a man in his forties, overweight, with a large belly and sagging breasts. His mouth is smallish and tight. Experts believe the portrait of Hemiunu to be accurate, as such statues of royal personages usually were. In describing the look of the statue, Egyptologist P. H. Newby describes Hemiunu as "one of considerable toughness, even ruthlessness."

Beyond the statue itself, little is known about Hemiunu. Yet an archaeological discovery made in the 1920s has developed into an interesting theory concerning Hemiunu. In 1925 George Andrew Reisner, an American archaeologist, was excavating at a Giza site. When the expedition photographer's tripod accidentally broke through a piece of masonry buried in the sand, an important discovery was made. Digging eighty feet down, Reisner's team uncovered the burial chamber of Hetepheres, the mother of Khufu.

But the royal sarcophagus, when opened, was empty. This created a puzzle for Reisner, for the tomb itself did not seem to have been invaded by thieves. If not, where was the body of the royal mother of Khufu? All that could be

contents have disappeared. Archaeologist Sir Flinders Petrie made note during his excavations that the sarcophagus is about an inch larger than the ascending corridor's opening. From this he concluded that the coffin was placed in the pyramid while it was under construction.

The work of archaeologist Colonel Howard-Vyse included breaking through the granite slabs resting above the burial chamber. While examining these upper chambers, his men discovered the only known references to the builder of this pyra-

found was a chest containing, according to Reisner, "the canopic packages [stone mummification jars] which contained the entrails of the queen; all that has survived of the mortal remains of the mother of Khufu." Reisner soon began to develop a theory about the missing queen.

Reisner's conjectures follow this course: When the queen died, she was probably not buried at the Giza site, but near the pyramid of her husband, Snefru, at Dahshur. After the royal center of activity was moved by her son to Giza, Dahshur became a target of tomb robbers, who vandalized her tomb, stealing away the gold and jewels, as well as the mummified remains of the queen. When the temple priests found the tomb violated and the royal corpse missing, they went to Hemi-

When archaeologists opened the sarcophagus of Khufu's mother they were surprised to find that although it was untouched by thieves, the coffin contained no corpse.

unu in a panic, lest the king discover their negligence. As Reisner's theory continues, Hemiunu probably informed the king of the robbers' violation of the tomb, but concealed from him the fact that his mother's body had been desecrated, or violated. Probably, Hemiunu suggested a new burial site for Hetepheres at Giza, where a tomb was carved, the burial rituals carried out, and a new sarcophagus interred, all without the benefit of a mummified body. Without Khufu's knowledge, his mother's new burial site never contained the one item it was supposed to: her mummified corpse.

mid. These stones, not intended for display, still bear the red ochre quarry marks that include the name of pharaoh Khufu.

These stone ceiling slabs are unique in pyramid construction. Mendelssohn explains their purpose:

The roof of the King's Chamber has no exact architectural parallel. Above its flat ceiling, which is composed of nine slabs weighing in aggregate [as a group] about 400 tons, there are five separate compartments, the ceilings of the first four being flat and the fifth having a

Khufu's empty sarcophagus, long before pillaged by tomb robbers, still sits in its chamber in the Great Pyramid.

pointed roof. The purpose of this construction, it appears, was to eliminate any risk of the ceiling of the chamber collapsing under the weight of the superincumbent [resting] masonry. Whether such extreme precautions were required by the character of the building may be debatable; they have, however, been justified by subsequent events. Every one of the massive slabs of granite in the ceiling of the chamber and many of those in the relieving compartments have been cracked—presumably by an earthquake—but none has yet collapsed.

CAPPING THE PYRAMID

While work on the interior tunnels and chambers continued in the center of the Khufu pyramid, the work on the outside continued. Workers continued to pile on layer after layer of stones. As the pyramid gained a height of, perhaps, three or four hundred feet, there was probably not enough room to allow for four ramps encircling the pyramid. Engineers cut the number to two ramps, using one as a path for stones up the pyramid's exterior, while the other served as a ramp for the work gangs to bring their empty sledges, ropes, and other equipment down.

When the final multistone layer had been set in place, the last stone, called a capstone, was dragged to the pyramid's summit. Such a stone resembled a small pyramid itself, having the same angle as the giant it would stand atop. Often such capstones were made of granite. As workers dragged the stone up, priests offered prayers and burned incense, blessing the event.

Once at the top, the capstone was removed from its sledge and placed on wooden blocks as the workers maneuvered the stone into position. The sledge was sent down the ramp. Carefully, the blocking was removed and the capstone slipped into place. A piece of stone extended from the cap-stone's underside. This protrusion was designed to keep the capstone in place and to provide a guide for setting the cap-stone so that it would align with the four sides of the pyramid. The priests continued their rituals, offering more prayers to their gods, as the scent of incense wafted over the summit of the nearly finished pyramid.

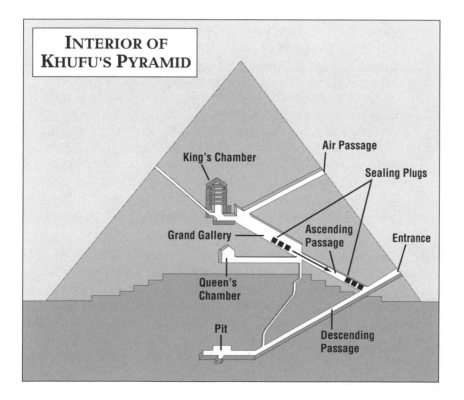

INTERIOR OF KHUFU'S PYRAMID

King's Chamber

Air Passage

Sealing Plugs

Grand Gallery

Ascending Passage

Entrance

Queen's Chamber

Pit

Descending Passage

SEALING THE PYRAMIDS

When the pharaoh's mummified remains were placed inside his tomb, the priests made their final exit from the burial chamber. But how did the priests manage to leave the pyramids alive and yet seal off the tomb and its contents from later tomb robbers?

The pyramid builders attempted to accomplish this through a series of ingenious construction methods. For example, to hide the entrances themselves when constructing the great monuments, such openings were disguised by making the stones blocking them look the same as any other casing stone. But more than once tomb robbers discovered the outer entrances and made their way into the pyramids.

When that occurred, the robbers faced a variety of blocks to their progress—literally. For one, the Egyptian architects included portcullises when constructing tunnels in the pyramids. A portcullis is a stone door or barrier. Such portcullises were placed in channels built at the top of a tunnel. Stone slabs were slipped vertically up into these channels and secured with ropes to keep them out of the tunnel until it needed sealing. Wooden logs were also placed under the stone barriers, to hold them up.

Once the interior work was finished in a pyramid and the pharaoh's body was entombed, the priests removed the wooden supports and cut the ropes, lowering the stone portcullises into place, blocking the tunnel. Several portcullises might be lowered in close succession in the same tunnel. The Great Pyramid featured three portcullises that were lowered to block the short tunnel between the Grand Gallery and the King's Chamber. Such portcullises

POLISHING THE PYRAMID'S EXTERIOR

Placing the capstone on the summit of each of these pyramids signified the end of their construction. However, there was still serious work to be done. I. E. S. Edwards describes the nature of the work remaining:

The laborious process of assembling the pyramid was now finished and work could be started on dressing the

were cut from granite, rather than limestone, to make it difficult for tomb robbers to break through them.

In addition, pyramid builders sometimes left stones inside the pyramid's larger rooms to be pushed into tunnels, thus blocking the way for future robbers. Several tunnel plugs were used in the Great Pyramid. After moving these blocks into place, the priests had to exit to the pyramid's outside by a special shaft just large enough for each of them to wriggle through. Despite such elaborate measures, tomb robbers eventually broke into each pyramid. Caliph al-Mamun's men, when they faced such things as granite tunnel plugs, simply dug into the tunnel's walls and chiseled through the softer limestone blocks, bypassing the intended blockades.

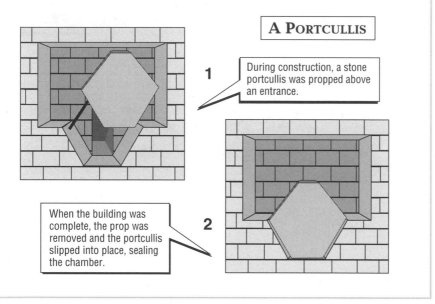

A PORTCULLIS

1 During construction, a stone portcullis was propped above an entrance.

When the building was complete, the prop was removed and the portcullis slipped into place, sealing the chamber. **2**

four outer faces, beginning with the capstone. As the work proceeded, the supply-ramp and the foot-hold embankments would be lowered, thus making fresh courses of casing-stones accessible for dressing. In order to complete the task more quickly, it is possible that the reduction of the ramp and embankments was not carried out gradually, but in layers of several feet;

Though the Great Pyramid no longer has its outer layer of brilliantly polished casing stones, the pyramid still stands as a testament to the grandeur of ancient Egypt.

wooden scaffolding would then be erected in their place so that a large number of men could be employed on different levels at the same time. Scaffolding was certainly known to the Egyptians, and the time saved by its use when dressing the five acres of casing on each face of the Great Pyramid, for example, would have been considerable.

Further work was required because of the need to smooth the exposed side of the outer casing stones, followed by a polishing, using abrasives, until the exterior of each pyramid at Giza shone brilliantly white across the sun-drenched Egyptian plateau.

EPILOGUE

Today the Pyramids of Giza stand as mute monuments to the efficiency of Egyptian engineering. While other great works of the ancient world have come and gone, the Pyramids continue to dominate the desert plain near the modern city of Cairo.

DESTRUCTION OVER THE CENTURIES

But the Pyramids have experienced abuse over the centuries. Forty-five centuries have come and gone since the completion of these great tombs. While they still survive, the Pyramids have suffered greatly over the millennia. The effects of weather, especially that of sand-carrying winds, have caused the stones of the Pyramids to erode. The mud brick mastabas and lesser pyramids surrounding the Pyramids of Giza have not weathered well, and many are in ruin. They have become challenging piles of rubble for curious archaeologists.

Michael D. Lemonick, writing for *Newsweek* magazine, describes how nature continues to deal harsh blows to the forty-five-hundred-year-old Giza monuments:

> Rubble and rock dust crumbling from the pyramid of Khafre have accumulated in piles on its lower levels. In the pyramid of Khufu, encrustations of salt, left by the evaporation of brackish groundwater, have eaten away at the walls of the burial chamber. The Sphinx . . . has lost a 600-lb chunk from its right shoulder, and the neck is so weak that the statue's massive head is in danger of falling off.

While nature acts on the pyramids, man has mistreated these ancient monuments, as well. Over time the pyramids lost their religious significance as tombs of great pharaohs. They became, for many Egyptians, just huge piles of stones that could be used to build other buildings. This is why the outer veneer of casing stones is largely missing from all three Pyramids. Khafre's pyramid has some casing stones still in place, but they are mostly found at the monument's peak.

During other ages, the Pyramids and the Sphinx have been abused by invaders. When the Turks invaded Egypt in the early 1500s, they used the Sphinx for target practice. In the late

For forty-five centuries the Pyramids of Giza have withstood the ravages of wind, heat, and destruction by humans.

1790s the French did the same under their great general, Napoleon Bonaparte, when his army campaigned across Egypt.

Since their construction, the Pyramids have faced the constant threat of violation by tomb robbers. All the Giza Pyramids were broken into at some time in the past. The treasures sealed away in their stone burial vaults are long gone. Tomb robbing generally took place during the reigns of weak pharaohs. Even though it was a crime punishable by death, the robbers continued their work, lured into the great tombs by the promise of fabulous riches, including jewels, gold, and precious stones, buried with the pharaoh.

Throughout the centuries nature, invading armies, and tomb robbers have caused the Giza Pyramids to suffer greatly. But today the greatest threat, perhaps, to these ancient monuments is from the Egyptian people themselves. Again, *Newsweek* reporter Lemonick gives a grim picture of the new realities on the Giza Plateau and how they affect the Pyramids:

> As the number of Egyptians increases, people have spilled out of the cities in search of housing. The Giza Plateau, once far from urban sprawl, now lies almost in

the shadow of modern apartment buildings. Nearby factories and old vehicles spew forth noxious clouds of particulate-laden exhaust, which becomes corrosive when dissolved by rain. Vibrations from traffic produce cracks in the monuments. More serious still is the damage caused by water. An estimated 80% of Cairo's incoming water supply escapes from leaking pipes into the ground. And the aging sewerage system, built . . . to serve a population of half a million, is choking on the wastes of 13 million. Much of the wastewater overflows into the soil. The resulting rise in the water table gradually undermines the foundations of buildings, causing them to list [tilt] and even collapse.

A PLACE FOR TOURISTS

A second population threat to the Pyramids is the approximately two million tourists from around the world who visit the Pyramids of Giza each year. They come to look at these giant monuments and, just as visitors have for thousands of years, they stand amazed. Many take tour buses up Pyramid Road to the tombs and find themselves in the very shadows of the limestone towers. Despite the official signs scattered at the bases of the Pyramids that read "It is Forbidden to Climb the Pyramid," tourists still clamber up their ancient, deteriorating slopes. These same tourists take excursions into the Great Pyramid of Khufu, never realizing the damage they may be causing. Experts explain that a group of tourists numbering fewer than ten who tour a tomb for an hour can raise the tomb's humidity by five percentage points. Such a rise in humidity causes increased growth in fungi, bacteria, and algae on the tomb's walls, causing more deterioration.

Close to two million tourists visit the Pyramids each year.

The Egyptian government is responding to many of these problems and spending millions of dollars in the process. Tons of sand and rubbish have been removed from the Giza Plateau in an effort to fight erosion, and Egyptologists are leading an effort to shore up some of the stones that are in the poorest condition at the base of the Khufu pyramid. New laws restrict cars from the pyramid site, as well as camel drivers and peddlers. Visitors to the ancient site now ride electric buses up from the city to the Giza Plateau. Archaeologists and engineers are working together to assess the portions of the Giza site that need attention in an attempt to halt future destruction.

Such changes in policy at Giza are greatly needed. Some of these restrictions and cautions may determine how tourists act once they arrive, but they continue to visit this monument site by the hundreds of thousands. Tourists continue to take guided tours into the Great Pyramid of Khufu. Through an entrance on the north side of the Pyramid, visitors may enter, guided through a narrow passage cut by, perhaps, the most famous tomb robber of them all, the Arabian caliph named al-Mamun. Down the descending passage, up another, into the Grand Gallery, where an occasional bat flits around the limestone ceiling, until finally the modern-day tourist finds himself or herself in the King's Chamber. There sits the ancient sarcophagus, empty. But visitors go away from the experience far from disappointed. They have visited another time and place, one like no other they will ever visit again. They have experienced the days of the pharaohs.

Outside, the hot winds blow, the sun beats down on ageless desert sands, and the shadows of the Pyramids extend across the Giza Plateau, as they have for hundreds of humanity's generations. Once upon a time the ancient world could boast of seven great wonders, built by the hands of man. Today only one remains, towering toward a cloudless Egyptian sky.

FOR FURTHER READING

Jeanne Bendick, *Egyptian Tombs*. New York: Franklin Watts, 1989.

Rosalie David and Antony E. David, *Ancient Egypt*. Warwick Press, 1984.

David Macaulay, *Pyramid*. Boston: Houghton Mifflin, 1975.

Barbara Mitchell, *Pyramids*. St. Paul: Greenhaven Press, 1988.

John Weeks, *The Pyramids: A Cambridge Topic Book*. Minneapolis: Lerner Publications, in cooperation with Cambridge University Press, 1977.

WORKS CONSULTED

Cyril Aldred, *The Egyptians*. New York: Thames and Hudson, 1984.

Lionel Casson, *Ancient Egypt*. New York: Time-Life Books, 1965.

I. E. S. Edwards, *The Pyramids of Egypt*. New York: Viking Press, 1972.

Farouk El-Baz, "Finding a Pharaoh's Funeral Bark," *National Geographic*, April 1988.

Evan Hadingham, "Pyramid Schemes," *Atlantic*, November 1992.

Alice J. Hall, "Legacy of a Dazzling Past," *National Geographic*, March 1977.

Michael D. Lemonick, "Perilous Times for the Pyramids," *Newsweek*, May 15 1989.

Jane McIntosh, *The Practical Archaeologist*. New York: Facts On File Publications, 1986.

Kurt Mendelssohn, *The Riddle of the Pyramids*. New York: Praeger Publishers, 1974.

Barbara Mertz, *Red Land, Black Land: Daily Life in Ancient Egypt*. New York: Dodd, Mead, 1978.

———, *Temples, Tombs and Hieroglyphs: A Popular History of Ancient Egypt*. New York: Dodd, Mead, 1978.

P. H. Newby, *The Egypt Story: Its Art, Its Monuments, Its People, Its History*. New York: Abbeville Press, 1979.

Rene Poirier, *Fifteen Wonders of the World*. New York: Random House, 1960.

David Roberts, "Age of Pyramids: Egypt's Old Kingdom," *National Geographic*, January 1995.

John Romer, *Ancient Lives: Daily Life in Egypt of the Pharaohs*. New York: Holt, Rinehart and Winston, 1984.

Desmond Stewart, *The Pyramids and Sphinx*. New York: Newsweek Book Division, 1971.

INDEX

PICTURE CREDITS

ABOUT THE AUTHOR

Tim McNeese received a bachelor's degree from Harding University in Searcy, Arkansas, and a master's degree in history from Southwest Missouri State University. He taught secondary-level history, English, and journalism for sixteen years, and is currently associate professor of history at York College.

He has written twenty books for young readers, including two eight-part series, *Americans on the Move* and *American Timeline*, and four books for the *Building History* series. He coedited the college texts *History in the Making: Sources and Essays of America's Past*, Volumes I and II.

Tim and his wife, Bev, live in York, Nebraska, with their daughter, Summer, and their son, Noah, who attends York College. They share their home with two Siamese cats and a cocker spaniel named Franklin. Tim enjoys woodworking, traveling, reading, and writing.